Holy by Nature

Kelly M Barnes

Published by Kelly M Barnes, 2024.

While every precaution has been taken in the preparation of this book, the publisher assumes no responsibility for errors or omissions, or for damages resulting from the use of the information contained herein.

HOLY BY NATURE

First edition. July 9, 2024.

Copyright © 2024 Kelly M Barnes.

ISBN: 979-8224393190

Written by Kelly M Barnes.

Preface

Struggling to overcome sin; Fighting off temptation; With clinched fists, daily contending with the "old man" or sin nature we inherited from Adam; Battling with sinful habits, addictions, attitudes, and tolerating things like sickness, lack, anxiety, depression, despair, fear, unbelief, etc. All of this is part of the believer's walk of faith on "this side of glory"; it's normal and even expected, but THANK GOD - at least we are saved and have the promise heaven and hope of eternal life! Until then, we can be glad Jesus holds our hands along the way, and when He brings us to glory one day, all of these struggles and fights will come to an end, right? Because it is their daily experience and reality, practically all Christians would fully agree with these statements, but this book will examine and challenge these assertions or beliefs. Indeed, there are battles to fight, and learning to walk in our identity in the Lord is surely a process, but many of our ongoing struggles are due to our lack of revelation or understanding, and especially due to many false and dangerous doctrines we have embraced. For instance, we've been taught that the Apostle Paul, who the Church considers one of the greatest believers who ever lived, said sin and evil dwelled within <u>him</u> (apparently even after his conversion), therefore causing him to struggle to overcome it, fighting and contending to "die daily" to it! So, we reason, we can be sure this will not only be *our* daily experience, but it will likely be even worse because we assume that none of us could walk with God like Paul or other biblical characters did!

This assessment of the believer's walk of faith is considered the "gospel truth" within the Church at large, and those who suggest this is <u>not</u> the "normal and expected" life of a Christian is said to be out of touch with reality *and* the Word of God – and even labeled a heretic. This reasoning is a perfect example of how our behavior is the fruit of our beliefs or inner convictions. This book will help you understand how all sin is more of a *belief* problem that a behavior problem, and that when we align our beliefs or convictions with what the Scriptures truly teach on this subject, our behavior will naturally and effortlessly change from the inside-out.

When it comes to this topic, there are three groups of believers: 1) those who <u>contend</u> with sin and temptation, striving to overcome it; 2) those who are <u>content</u> to live with sin because they have either lost hope or because they abuse the grace of God; and 3) those who realize they have already <u>conquered</u> or overcome the world, the enemy, and the war against sin and temptation by their union with Christ, and have entered into the rest of God as a result. Using Scripture alone, this book will not only show you what is possible, but what is God's original and perfect will or design for you in the HERE and NOW. But no worries – we aren't going to cut sin and temptation out of the equation altogether. This book does not suggest the idea that Christians no longer have the "freedom" or ability to sin or give in to temptation just because they are born-again or saved, nor imply that a true believer *can't* or *doesn't* ever struggle to overcome these things. But here are the questions: *why* do most struggle with besetting sin, along with things such as sickness, disease, fear, lack, emotional pain, etc.? Must we accept as "fact" that such things are "normal" and "expected" for us? Does Scripture truly teach, as most Christians believe, that until we physically die, we "have no choice" but to tolerate or struggle with these things and live in sin's grip? If not, how would it even be *possible* for us to live any other way – as long as we are confined to these "earthen vessels" we call a body? With a teachable heart, along with an open Bible, explore these questions with me and be prepared to have your mind re-wired and renewed by the Word of God, and your life transformed as a result!

This book is loaded with Scripture that affirms its contents, but you will read some things you haven't read or heard, and you may wonder, "Where is *that* in the Bible?" But keep this in mind: If New Covenant truths and realities were shared with saints while they still lived under the Old Covenant, they would have said, *"Where's that in the Law and Prophets?"* They simply had no grid for where God was going to take His people and for what He was going to do through His Son, so He kept it "hidden" within types and shadows. As He said to His disciples, Jesus would say to us who are joined to Him under the New Covenant: *"To you it has been granted to know the mysteries of the kingdom; Blessed are the eyes which see the things you see, for I say to you, that many prophets and kings wished to see the things which you see, and did not see them, and to hear the things which you hear, and did not hear them."* (See Rom.16:25-26; 1 Cor.2:7-14; Eph.3:8-10; Col.1:25-27). Without doubt, God's Word is our *only* standard and plumbline for truth, and we are to test all doctrine with the Word – if something contradicts or conflicts with what God has said, we must readily reject it. However, it is important to understand that because revelation is progressive in nature, not everything God has yet to reveal to His people concerning His kingdom and our inheritance will be explicitly taught in His Word. Even Jesus said to His disciples that He had many more truths He wanted to share with them, but He *couldn't* because they weren't ready to hear and receive it. This is one of the reasons He sent His Holy Spirit to indwell us, so that He would teach and guide us into all the truth (see John 16:12-13). "Guiding us into all truth" clearly implies a process whereby the Lord progressively "pulls back the veil" to reveal greater insight concerning the kingdom and our inheritance – things which have always belonged to us, but we just didn't see or understand them.

So, when we hear something that doesn't have a specific Bible verse to back it up, the first thing we must do is test it to Scripture, making sure it doesn't contradict it or oppose the nature of God. If it doesn't, that obviously <u>doesn't</u> mean we should accept it as truth – the point is, we should not immediately label it "false teaching" because Scripture is silent on the topic or doesn't address the topic directly. In other words, just because something is *extrabiblical* does not automatically make it <u>un</u>biblical or false teaching. How will we know if something is from God or not? That's easy – the Lord said if we desire to know and do His will, we will recognize true teaching when we hear it (John 7:17). He also said that if we are pursuing God and His kingdom above all things, we can trust His Spirit to give us discernment so that we may distinguish between truth and error (see Luke 12:32; Matt.6:33, 7:7-11).

One last note: throughout this book, God's Hebrew names, Yahweh and Yeshua will be used, rather than the transliterated names, "God" and "Jesus." This is <u>not</u> because He turns a deaf ear to such terms, but because calling Him by His true name shows more reverence, as He says His Name is to be *revered* and held in *high esteem*, and that in the Last Days, His Name will be *known* (Ex.3:15, Mal.3:16,4:2, Is.52:6, Zec.14:9). In Hebrew, Yahweh means "to be" (referring to His eternality as the "I Am") and Yeshua means "Yahweh is salvation."

CHAPTER 1

It All Began in the Garden

Lies and deception. It all began in the Garden. Satan wasted no time, using lies to persuade the first two human beings not only to question the heart of their Creator and Father, but also their identity and purpose. Our Enemy, who Yeshua [Jesus] called the "Father of Lies," has always used deception to bring us into a place of spiritual ignorance and blindness, which in turn brings bondage and captivity on many levels. As we read in Jeremiah 16:9, *...the Gentiles shall come to you from the ends of the earth, saying, "Surely our fathers have inherited lies, worthless and unprofitable things." *There is a reason why deception is Satan's choice weapon and modus operandi. He may not be wise, but he is *not* stupid, for our enemy knows that if God's people ever catch revelation of who they truly are, he is finished! There *will* come a time when that happens, but until then, his primary objective is not only to confuse us and keep us in ignorance, but to convince us of outright lies concerning the nature of our heavenly Father, as well as our identity and destiny in Him. In Matthew chapter 4, we read that Satan even tried to tempt Yeshua into questioning *His* identity during His time in the wilderness, asking Him several times, "IF You are the Son of God...". If he did this with our Messiah, how much more would he try to have us question who we are as God's sons and daughters? Satan knows that out of identity flows vision, purpose, hope, and empowerment, which means the opposite is also true: when our understanding of our true identity becomes lost or obscured, we not only lose sight of our purpose and direction, but begin to live with a sense of hopelessness and despair. As our sense of purpose and direction is lost, life begins to feel bored and empty, and in our efforts to find meaning and fulfillment, we pursue things which lead us into various forms of captivity. Yahweh says in Hosea 4:6 and Isaiah 5:13 say that His people *perish* and *go into exile* for lack of knowledge; lack of knowledge of what? His Word or Law (which surely includes spiritual laws He established). And Proverbs 29:18 says, *where there is no vision* [revelation], *the people cast off restraint.*

False doctrine or lies and ignorance are precisely why most Christians have lost their vision or sense of purpose and are suffering from a major identity crisis. The truth is, most of us as believers have *never* known or had a revelation of our true identity in the Lord. I believe I've barely scratched the surface of this myself, but I am excited about where the Lord is taking His Body in these Last Days as He prepares us for His return! But ignorance or lack of revelation is why so many Christians are battling with sin and addiction, as well as emotional, physical, and relational pain and suffering – *and* believing that is not only normal, but expected. One reason why the Church is in such a state of bondage and immaturity is because most Christians have been taught a distorted and unscriptural view of God's sovereignty. When we say Yahweh is "sovereign," that means He has *supreme power* and *authority*. However, many believe it also means or implies *control* (as in manipulation and coercion). While the Lord has all power and authority, and while His Spirit certainly influences people and events, contrary to popular belief, He does *not* "control" everyone and everything like a Puppeteer. But many Christians have come to believe that because Yahweh is "sovereign," that means His will, desire or plan for their life will most assuredly come to pass – no matter what. An entire book could be written to address this topic, but Scripture makes it very clear that the Lord has given us the freedom of choice and has commanded us to steward our lives well by walking in wisdom, discipline, and responsibility. His destiny or plans for us do <u>not</u> unfold or come to pass automatically simply because we are born-again or because we belong to Him. The Bible is full of examples of God's people failing to fulfill their calling in Him or living out their purpose and identity in Him – while paying a high price for it! If God's will or a believer's destiny *always* comes to pass, then Scripture wouldn't say things such as "do not be foolish, but understand what the will of the Lord is," and "Make sure no one misleads or deceives you" (Eph.5:17; Matt.24:4; 1 John 3:7).

Another reason why the Church is in such a state of bondage and immaturity is because most believers are taught to never question or test the doctrinal positions of their pastors or spiritual leaders, and if they do, they are quickly labeled "rebellious" or accused of having a "Jezebel spirit." And because most believers have never been to seminary or Bible college, they feel they are unqualified to question the doctrines of the Church or their pastor. Besides, the average Christian assumes it is not *their* responsibility, but their *pastor's* responsibility or job to know the Bible and "rightly divide" it. But this pushes the issue back further – as most seminary students do not question or test the validity of what *they* were taught either. If it weren't for the verses quoted above, we would likely reject the idea that *false doctrine* could be the primary reason we see so much sin, pain, and suffering in the Body of Christ. But the apostle Paul sternly warned us about false teaching in Acts 20:29: *I know that after my departure, savage wolves will come in among you, not sparing the flock, and from among your own selves' men will arise, speaking <u>perverse</u> things, to <u>draw away the disciples</u> after them. Therefore, <u>be on the alert</u>.* And we read in 2 Peter 3:17:.....<u>*be on your guard*</u> *so that you are not carried away by the <u>error</u> of unprincipled men and <u>fall</u> from your own steadfastness.* Even our Messiah *commands* us not to allow others to deceive us, as He said in Matthew 24:4, *"<u>See to it</u> that no one misleads you."*

How do we fulfill that responsibility? Even from the beginning, we read that Yahweh established parameters by which we differentiate between truth and falsehood – parameters that will never change because His Word is everlasting (Deut.4:2,12:32, ch.13; Ps.89:34, 119:89). Our heavenly Father tells us to *test* or *examine* _everything_ *carefully, to* _pay close attention_ *to your teaching....for in doing so, you will save both yourself and your hearers,* and to *be careful how we hear or listen* (1 Thess.5:21; 1 Tim.4:6; Luke 8:18). Of course, we cannot trust in our own discernment or judgment to do this, as we read in 2 Timothy 1:14, *Guard,* _through the Holy Spirit_ *who indwells us, the treasure which has been entrusted to you.* In other words, we shouldn't accept everything we hear from a pastor or teacher as the "gospel truth," rather, we should test and examine it to make sure it aligns with Scripture. This is precisely what the Berean believers did in Acts 17 when they heard Paul's teaching. They didn't receive it as the truth until they were able to *validate* it by comparing it with the Scriptures (in this case, the Law and Prophets, the only "scripture" they had at that time). So, before we delve into this topic, we must understand that we are personally responsible to be the "gatekeepers" of our hearts and minds. The Lord does not do this for us; *we* must do this, of course, by His Holy Spirit who "guides us into all the truth," as He promised He would (2 Tim.1:14; John 14:26, 16:13). And we need not be afraid, as Yeshua said, *"_Fear not_, little flock, for it is the Father's _good pleasure_ to _give_ you the kingdom."* He said that if we ask, we *shall receive*; if we seek we *shall find*; if we knock, the door *shall be opened,* and that if we ask for bread, *He will give it to us* - not a snake or scorpion – meaning He will guard us from deception (John 14:26,16:23; Luke 12:32,11:9-13).

There are *dozens* of damaging lies God's people have learned and embraced throughout the ages, including whole systems of doctrine such as Dispensationalism and Cessationism. In a nutshell they teach that God replaced Israel, His chosen people, with the Gentile nations (who gave birth to the Church Age), and that miracles/ signs/wonders, along with supernatural encounters and the miraculous gifts of the Spirit, were withdrawn from the Church at the close of the 1st Century. But these false doctrines were concocted by man and passed along to us, again, as Jeremiah 16:9b says, *"Our fathers have inherited nothing but lies, worthless things in which there is no profit."* However, this book will not focus on dismantling such beliefs or systems of doctrines, but on the destructive lies concerning our *identity* as sons and daughters of God who have *truly* been set free from sin and have been made righteous. One of the biggest lies Satan has sold believers is that they are "saved sinners" or "sinful saints." There is a reason why such terms sound contradictory, much like a "married bachelor" or an "honest liar." But such terminology has been labeled and embraced by the Church as "paradoxes of the Faith," not contradictions - or so we've been told. Surely there are many paradoxes in our walk of faith. For instance, we live or find life when we "die" to ourselves; we are the greatest in the kingdom of God if we become the *least* (a servant) of all; the more we give and humble or empty ourselves, the more we receive and become exalted (in spirit and/or physically), etc. But pairing the words *sinful* with "saint" and *saved* with "sinner" is not only unbiblical, but <u>contradictory</u>, *not* paradoxical. As we proceed, we will clearly see from a biblical standpoint, *sinners* are sinful, not saints, while *saints* are saved and sanctified, not sinners!

Having said that, let me quickly make the disclaimer that this book does <u>not</u> promote the false teaching of Perfectionism, which says that because believers are indwelt by the Holy Spirit and are new creations in Christ, it means they are literally or physically *perfect, flawless* or *sinless*; neither does it mean they are <u>unable</u> to sin, will *never* sin, or at times make ungodly, foolish choices (like Adam and Eve did in their pre-fallen state). The Lord would have to revoke our free will for that to happen! So, please keep this in mind as you continue reading. Using Scripture alone, my objective is to show that we <u>cannot</u> be a truly born-again believer while still *practicing* sin or leading a sinful life, where sinning is routine, normal, and even *expected* because, "after all, we're only human." This book will challenge the widely accepted belief that true believers are "sinners" or "wretches saved by grace" who sin "all the time" and are bound to struggle with sin and temptation all their lives "this side of glory." This perspective or belief comes in a variety of flavors, and here are just a few you may have heard and believed. Please note: some of these beliefs reflect biblical truth to a degree, but this book will use Scripture to expose and address the false and dangerous implications and assertions behind them:

> *"Christians aren't perfect, just forgiven."*

> *"Because we are sinners and only human, we can't help but sin, and until we leave this earth, we'll always be fighting to overcome the evil desires of our sinful nature."*

> *"We 'miss the mark' all the time.....we're likely sinning all the time but just don't realize it."*

> *"Sin no longer has dominion over our lives as Christians, but we're 'sinners' like everyone else. The difference is that our sins are covered by the blood of Christ."*

> *"True spiritual maturity is measured by how aware we are of our sinfulness and depravity."*

> *"The closer we draw near to God, the more we see how corrupt, depraved, and rotten we are."*

> *"Believers are 'sinful saints': we're rotten to the core, but by the blood, holy to the Lord!"*

> *"Christians are just 'sinners' saved by grace!"*

> *"The only thing you need to do to be saved is believe in Jesus and confess Him as Lord and Savior."*

> *"God's Law is not only hard to keep, but impossible – which is why Jesus replaced it with the 'Law of Love.'"*

> *"In Christ, we live under grace, not law, which means God no longer holds us accountable for sin."*

> *"My sin no longer offends or grieves God because He sees me through 'blood-stained' glasses."*

I could list several other examples, but if you were led to believe such things, get your Bible out and hold on to your seats – because we are going to examine such teachings or mentalities to see if they truly hold up to the full counsel of God's Word. Many Christians would say, *"Of course God's Word teaches such beliefs - just read your Bible!"* Let me repeat: there are kernels of truths in statements like these and we can find verses which, when taken out of context or read as stand-alone verses, support such views. For example, Romans 10:9 indeed says we are "saved" by confessing Jesus as Lord and believing in His resurrection, and Ephesians 2:8-9 clearly tells us *how* we are saved: *by grace and not works*, but if we read such verses in a vacuum and not compare them with the *full counsel* of Scripture on the nature of true faith and salvation, we will come away with beliefs that are not only antithetical or contrary to the Word as a whole, but flat out heretical, falling under the category of what Paul referred to as "doctrines of demons" (1 Tim.4:1).

Some may see this as a matter of semantics or believe the terminology we use is a trivial matter that has little to no consequences, but this is <u>not</u> about semantics or word games. You will see that what we believe and say about ourselves is extremely important and has a profound impact on our daily lives as believers. You will also likely notice that I am redundant throughout this book, but that is intentional, as repetition will help the truth take root in your heart. And as you can already tell in the first two pages of this book, we are going to hit the Scriptures hard because they are the only standard by which we discern truth from error and by which we test all doctrine - so there will be no apology for quoting "too much" Scripture.

So again, as the Bereans tested Paul's teaching with the Scriptures, we are going to use the Word of God to test the belief that we can be a born-again believer in Christ and still label ourselves a "saved sinner" or "sinful saint." In other words, does the Bible truly teach that believers are some strange hybrid, like a spiritual "Jekyll and Hyde," who have no choice but to live in a perpetual state of conflict or tension caused by two equally opposing natures that exist within them? Most Christians would say YES – using the Bible to support the belief that while we may be "born-again, new creations" who are *declared* holy and righteous, we nevertheless have no choice but to struggle with the sin-loving, carnal nature we inherited from Adam. One of the most popular passages of Scripture used to support this is Romans chapter 7, where Paul speaks of two opposing natures within humanity, where one nature wants to obey and please God, while the other nature wants to rebel against Him and live fleshly or carnal. It is my conviction that due to false teaching which has been passed down to us, albeit unwittingly, Romans 7 is one of the most misunderstood, distorted, and abused passages of Scripture that has led to disastrous consequences in the lives of believers. Before we examine and address Romans 7, let us look at a few key scriptures used in efforts to affirm these damaging beliefs or lies mentioned above. We will start with the Old Testament, which most Christians believe is obsolete (unless of course it supports their doctrinal paradigm, as in this case):

Genesis 6:5: *Then the Lord saw that the <u>wickedness of man</u> was great in the earth, and that every intent of the thoughts of his heart was <u>only evil continually</u>.*

Isaiah 64:6: *For all of us have become like one who is <u>unclean</u>, and all our righteous acts are like <u>filthy rags</u>; <u>all</u> of us wither like a leaf, and like the wind, <u>our sins sweep us away</u>.*

Jeremiah 17:9: *The <u>heart is deceitful</u> [sick] above all things <u>and desperately corrupt</u>;*

Proverbs 28:26a: *He who trusts in his own heart is a <u>fool</u>.*

Psalms 14:2-3: *The Lord has looked down from heaven upon the sons of men to see if there are any who understand, who seek after God. They have <u>all</u> turned aside, together they have become <u>corrupt</u>; There is <u>no one who does good, not even one</u>.* (Apostle Paul quotes these verses in Rom.3:10-12). [1]

And here are a few New Testament verses used:

1 John 1:8: *If we say we have <u>no sin</u>, we <u>deceive ourselves</u> and the truth is not in us.*

Matthew 15:19-20a: *"For <u>out of the heart come evil</u> thoughts, murder, adultery, sexual immorality, theft, false witness, and slander. These are the things which <u>defile</u> the man."*

Mark 2:17: *"Those who are well have no need of a physician, but those who are <u>sick</u>. For I came not to call the righteous, but <u>sinners</u>."*

I Timothy 1:15: *Christ came into the world to save <u>sinners</u>, of who <u>I am the worst</u>.*

Romans 3:10-12: *There is <u>none</u> righteous, not even one; there is none who understands, who seeks for God; all have turned aside, together they have become useless; there is <u>none</u> who does good, there is not even one.* (quoting Psalm 53).

Romans 7: *....the Law is spiritual, but I am of <u>flesh</u>, sold into <u>bondage to sin</u>; for I know that nothing good dwells in me, that is, in my flesh, for the wishing is present in me, but the doing of the good is not; but if I am doing the very thing I do not wish, I am no longer the one doing it, but <u>sin which dwells in me</u>.*

There are a lot more verses used (or <u>misused</u>) to support the belief that born-again believers are "sinners" or "sinful saints" who "sin all the time," but these examples should suffice. However, it is vital to understand that the verses quoted above from the *Old Testament* (along with Paul's quote of Psalm 53) are <u>not</u> talking about born-again new creations in Yeshua who have been co-crucified with Him, baptized in His Spirit, liberated from sin, and who share in His nature and resurrection power; such verses refer to *the fallen nature of man in his unredeemed, unregenerate, spiritually blind, and dead state.* 2 Corinthians 5:17 clearly affirms this by stating that if we are in Yeshua, the old has *passed away* and ALL things have become NEW, and that we are a totally NEW creature – which means our heart is no longer sick, deceitful, and corrupt, and we are no longer "obligated" to sin or controlled by a sin nature! If our heart is corrupt, evil, sick, and deceived, then according to Scripture, we are *not* a born-again new creation and we will <u>not</u> see God or inherit His kingdom. If we, as blood-bought saints of God who share in His nature, believe we are a "wretch" with a heart that is deceptive, dark, and impure, we are clearly disagreeing with our heavenly Father and actually agreeing with Satan, the father of lies and accuser of the brethren! That might sound harsh, but look at what our Father and Creator says:

Matthew 5:8: *"Blessed are the <u>pure in heart</u>, for <u>they shall see God</u>."*

1 John 3:3: *Everyone who thus hopes in Him <u>purifies himself</u> as He is pure.*

Hebrews 10:22: *Let us draw near with a <u>true heart</u> in full assurance of faith, with our <u>hearts sprinkled clean</u> from an evil conscience...*

1 Peter 1:22; 2:9: *Since you have <u>purified your souls</u> in obeying the truth through the Spirit in sincere love of the brethren, love one another fervently with a <u>pure heart</u>;*

But you are a chosen race, a <u>royal priesthood</u>, a <u>holy</u> nation, a people for God's own possession, that you may proclaim the excellencies of Him who called you out of darkness into His marvelous <u>light</u>.

Luke 6:45: *"A <u>good</u> man, out of the <u>good treasure</u> of his heart brings forth <u>good</u>....."*

Yes, the Lord accused His hearers in Matthew 7:11 that they were "evil," but He couldn't have been saying *every* human is evil because He also says there are "good" people, as in the verse above. And of course, the only way a person can become a "good" man or woman is when they become a "new creation" in Christ - saved, cleansed and transformed by His indwelling Spirit. But what about the verses we just read in Jeremiah and Psalms that say the human heart is *sick, deceitful,* or *wicked,* that <u>none</u> are "good," and that "have *all* turned aside and are corrupt"?! Yes, but as we can see from the verses we just read, we must be careful to read Scripture within its context and in light of prophetic fulfillment. Just as realtors say the three most important things concerning real estate are *location, location, location,* so we could say the three most important things concerning correct biblical interpretation are *context, context, context.* There are hundreds of awesome Bible verses we should claim over our lives, and we <u>should</u> pray the Word of God because it is very powerful, but did you know there are some scriptures that a born-again, Spirit-filled believer should <u>not</u> pray? For instance, we should *not* pray like David did in the Psalms, *"Take not Thy Holy Spirit from me,"* or ask the Lord not to forsake or abandon us. Why? Because such prayers ignore and even dishonor what Yeshua accomplished on our behalf and what He promised us - that He would send His Spirit to *permanently* indwell us, make us one with Him, and to *never* leave us (John 14:16; 1 Cor.6:17; Matt.28:20; Heb.13:5). Neither should we pray as Isaiah prayed in chapter 64, *"Rend the heavens and come down."* Luke 3:21 explicitly says "heaven was *opened"* when the Holy Spirit descended upon Yeshua as a dove, and when the "veil" of His flesh was torn at Calvary and the Spirit of God came to indwell believers on Pentecost, the kingdom of heaven was ushered into our hearts and into the earth (Luke 17:21)! And read what Yahweh prophesied through the prophet Jeremiah - the *same* prophet who said the heart of mankind is *sick* and *deceitful*:

Jeremiah 32:39-40: *"I will give them <u>one heart</u> and <u>one way</u>, that <u>they may fear Me always</u> for their own good....I will put the <u>fear</u> of Me in their hearts so that <u>they will not turn away</u> from Me."*

The prophet Ezekiel affirms this in **Ezekiel 36:26:** *"I will give you a <u>new heart</u> and put a <u>new spirit</u> within you; I will take the heart of stone out of your flesh and give you a <u>heart of flesh</u>. And I will <u>put My Spirit within you</u> and <u>cause you to walk in My statutes</u> and be <u>careful to obey</u> my laws."*

Yes, these prophecies are specifically referring to Israel, but if you have even a basic knowledge of the Bible, you will know that Yahweh sees a <u>non</u>-Israelite the same way He sees a *native-born* Israelite. The Scriptures, from the Old Testament to the New, clearly say there is "neither Jew nor Gentile in Christ" and that God sees all believers, regardless of their ethnicity, as those who have been grafted into the Olive Tree of His chosen nation Israel and have become one with them (Num.15:15-16; Gal.3:28; Rom.2:28-29,11:17). The point here is that through our Messiah and His indwelling Spirit, our hearts or spirits are now "new," "pure," "true," and "clean." This is exactly what it means to become a "new" creation in Christ, to be "born-again" or spiritually regenerated and resurrected. We often say as believers that our sins are "covered by the blood," but Yeshua did not merely "cover" our sin as the animal sacrifices under the first covenant temporarily did; He _removed_ our sin and _rendered our old man dead and powerless_, as Romans 6:6 says _our old self was crucified with Him, that our body of sin might be done away with_ [expiated, removed, and made powerless], _that we should no longer be slaves to sin_. We will later discuss in more detail the topic of our sins being "covered" by the blood of Yeshua.

But what about 1 John 1:8, which clearly says we "deceive" ourselves if we say we "have no sin"? This verse is used by many Christians to excuse or justify _habitual_ sin and disobedience in their lives. But John is _not_ saying we deceive ourselves by denying that we sin "all the time," _routinely,_ and _habitually,_ rather, he is saying we deceive ourselves by denying sin altogether. This isn't conjecture, as he says just a few verses later: _"I am writing these things to you so that you may NOT sin, and IF anyone sins_ [not when, but IF], _we have an Advocate with the Father, Jesus Christ, the righteous._ The first question and objection we might ask is, who would ever deny their sin _altogether_ or _period?_ I have personally met people on an overseas mission trip who have done just that, but as I continued to share the Gospel with them, it became apparent that they had no biblical understanding of the word "sin" or thought it only applied to terribly debase or vile people like murderers, rapists, thieves, etc. This shows how important it is that we understand spiritual concepts or principles that reflect biblical truth and not based on hearsay or man's opinion.

It is also very important that we understand the cultural and historical context of any scriptures we are reading or studying. At the time of John's writings, the teachings of Gnosticism were prevalent. Just as they are various "flavors" or versions of Christianity (denominations that differ on certain doctrines), so there were (and are) variations of Gnosticism. One of the common beliefs of Gnosticism is the false assertion that the material or physical realm is totally separate from the immaterial or spiritual realm. As a result of this belief, Gnostics conclude that because our spirits are holy or pure, and because God only cares about the spiritual (another false assertion), living an ungodly or immoral life with our *physical* body is inconsequential or irrelevant. Many took it to extremes by saying that because we are perfect and holy before God *spiritually* through faith in the Messiah, sin is not only a non-issue as far as He is concerned, it is not even real or doesn't exist! So, when John says, *"if we say <u>we have no sin</u>,"* he is saying we can't even be redeemed or saved because Yeshua only died for *sinners* or those who *acknowledge* they need a Savior because they have *sinned* against Him. Does this help you see the importance of understanding the cultural and historical context of Scripture? We don't have to go to seminary or become a Bible scholar or historian to understand these things, as there is a plethora of Bible study tools available to help us in our study. The question is, will we do just that: *study*, "to show ourselves approved to God, handling accurately the Word of truth," as opposed to casually reading or perusing Scripture? And more than anything, we should ask the Holy Spirit to guide and teach us as we study the Word, trusting Him to grant us revelation and understanding (as opposed to approaching the Bible as a mere textbook).

Another question we may ask is, isn't John addressing *born-again believers* in his letter and not unbelievers? Yes, the context of his letters makes it very clear that he is addressing those who are born-again, but as we know to be the case, not everyone who *claims* or *professes* to be born-again is truly born-again; not everyone who claims or believes to be members of the true Church are true members of Yeshua's body, <u>and</u> not everyone who *is* born-again or redeemed has their mind renewed through the knowledge of truth concerning the nature of faith and salvation. This is why he includes warnings in his writings, letting his audience know that if they claim to be without sin (period), or claim to know God but hate their brother or do not keep His commands, they are a *liar* and the truth is not in them – because *we know we have come to truly know Him IF we KEEP His commands,* and *if we say we abide in Him, we will walk in the <u>same</u> manner as HE walked* (2:4-6, 4:20-21). We see such warnings all throughout Paul's writings, especially to the "carnal" Christians in Corinth, and Peter also exhorts us to make "our calling and election sure" or certain by examining ourselves and our faith (e.g., affirming that our profession of faith naturally and increasingly manifests itself in our daily lives, producing fruit that aligns with His Word and nature).

Having said this, is John saying that if we are truly born-again, we will *flawlessly* or *perfectly* keep Yahweh's commands as Yeshua did? I suppose that is in the realm of possibility, but who would actually pull that off – even by the power of the Holy Spirit? Just because a believer has the Spirit's power available to them doesn't mean they will fully rely on Him and keep in step with Him 24/7. So, John is likely <u>not</u> saying this, which explains why he said Yeshua is our Advocate IF we sin![2] The question is, are we *characterized* as those who live obedient and righteous lives, or disobedient, sinful, and unrighteous lives? Has a genuine inward transformation taken place that outwardly manifests itself through an *increasingly* obedient, holy, and godly life? Biblically, we cannot call ourselves a Christian or a disciple of Yeshua while insisting we are still "wretched sinners."

Paul indeed labeled himself the "chief of sinners," but the context of his writings clearly show he was referring to his life *before* conversion, not after. If Paul was saying he was a sinner, let alone the *worst* of sinners, even *after* he came to faith, he would have negated his primary message that those who are in Yeshua are *new creations* who have been *freed* from sin; he would have contradicted the whole purpose of Yeshua's sacrifice and His message that believers are *rescued* from sin's dominion, *filled* with the HOLY Spirit, and therefore *empowered* and *inspired* to naturally <u>keep</u> God's laws and live righteously! Yes, Paul also said of himself in Romans 7:24, "wretched man that I am," but we will address that passage of Scripture later.

CHAPTER 2

Biblically Defining Sin & Repentance

If we are going to be discussing biblical words or terminology, it only makes sense to derive our understanding of them from the Lord and His Word. Let us begin with the term "sin." The first time the Bible uses this word is in Genesis 4:7: *....if you do not do well, <u>sin</u> lies and the door, and its desire is for you, but you should rule over it.* The Hebrew word for sin is *chattah,* a derivative of *chata.* Chattah means "offense," and chata means to "fail or to miss the way." This is likely how the Church has come to define sin as "missing the mark." Paul gives us a similar meaning of sin in Romans 6:23, where he says we have "fallen short of God's glory" and that the ultimate "wages" or payment for our sin is death. But this begs the question: what are we "falling short of," and what "way" or "mark" are we missing? Certainly it would be God's commandments, but violating His law is the by-product of a higher "mark" that we miss, and that is the glory of God within our true <u>identity</u> in Him. Remember, the Word says we are fashioned in His image and likeness, that He has crowned us with His glory, and that He IS our glory (Gen.1:26; Ps.8:5,3:3). So, when we "miss" that mark of our identity or don't know who we are in Him, we will inevitably fall short of His glory and miss the mark of His Word or ways. In other words, *a distorted or marred identity leads to distorted or wrong behavior*, an idea that will be discussed in more detail in the proceeding chapters. But does the Bible give us a definition of sin? Yes, and it is found in 1 John 3:4 and 5:17a: *Whoever commits sin also commits lawlessness, and <u>sin is lawlessness</u>; all unrighteousness is sin.* What is "unrighteousness"? Clearly anything that violates God's nature and Law, which reflect and *define* what it right, good, and holy (Deut.4:8; Ps.119:75,137,160; Rom.7:12). The Webster's version says *sin is the transgression* [violation] *of the law*. With this understanding, let us look at a few examples of how the Bible defines and refers to "sinners":

Psalms 1:1: *Blessed is the man who walks not in the counsel of the wicked, nor stands in the way of sinners, nor sits in the seat of scoffers; the wicked will not stand in the judgment, nor sinners in the congregation of the righteous.*

Psalms 104:35: *Let sinners be consumed from the earth and let the wicked be no more!* NOTE: Psalms use the terms, "sinner" and "wicked," interchangeably.

Isaiah 13:9, 65:20b: *Behold, the day of the Lord comes, cruel, with wrath and fierce anger, to make the land a desolation and to destroy its sinners from it!; For the child shall die one hundred years old, but the sinner being one hundred years old shall be accursed.*

Amos 9:10: *All the sinners of My people shall die by the sword...* [3].

John 9:31: *"We know that God does not listen to sinners, but if anyone is a worshipper of God and does His will, God listens to him."* These words were spoken by a common man who Yeshua healed, but look at what the Scriptures say on the topic:

Hebrews 7:26: *For it was indeed fitting that we should have such a high priest, holy, innocent, unstained, separated from sinners, and exalted above the heavens.* This verse refers to our Lord, but as His disciples, we are told that whoever is joined to Him is ONE spirit with Him, that we *share* in His divine nature, and that as He IS, so are we in THIS world! (2 Pet.1:4; 1 John 4:17; I Cor.6:17). And when the author of Hebrews speaks of being "called out" and "separate from sinners" he is quoting from Isaiah 52:11, which Paul likewise quotes in the verse below:

2 Cor.6:17: *"....come out from among them and be separate, says the Lord; do not touch any unclean thing, and I will welcome you."*

1 Pet.3:12, 4:18: *For the eyes of the Lord are toward the righteous, and His ears attend to their prayer, but the face of the Lord is <u>against</u> those <u>who do evil</u>. If it is with difficulty that the righteous is saved, what will become of the <u>godless</u> man and the <u>sinner</u>?* (Peter, who is writing *after* Calvary, agrees with David, directly quoting Psalm 34 and 66).

Rev.18:4: *"<u>Come out</u> of her My people, lest you share in her sins and receive of her plagues."*

Lev.11:44: *"I Am the Lord your God; <u>consecrate</u> yourselves and <u>be holy</u>, for I Am holy."* Peter quotes this verse in 1 Pet.1:15-16)

At this point, many would object to the Old Testament verses: *"That is OLD Testament or the OLD covenant – we are under a NEW covenant and under <u>grace</u>, not law, and our holiness before God isn't about the physical but the spiritual."* First of all, we must understand that all behavior is an outward expression of our perceived identity, meaning that how we live is the fruit of what's transpiring in our spirit-man. Secondly, it is true that we are no longer "under law" and are now "under grace" (Rom.6:14), and it *is* true that the <u>only</u> righteousness that justifies us and makes us truly acceptable before God comes <u>not</u> by keeping His laws but by *faith* in Yeshua. However, being "under grace and not law" *does not* mean God's Law is obsolete and that our lives no longer need to reflect its righteousness (we will later examine in more detail what Paul meant by this statement). But the truth is, <u>all</u> of us as God's people, before *and after* Yeshua came, are *commanded* to live a holy life, forsake sin, and separate ourselves from the world and its desires. The Old and New Testaments are in total harmony, as *both* of these verses from Isaiah 52 and Leviticus 11 are quoted by Paul, Peter, and John in the verses above. If you insist on labeling yourself a "sinner," look at what Yeshua says about you in

Luke 6:32-33: *"If you love those who love you, what benefit is that to you? For even <u>sinners</u> love those who love them.....if you do good to those who do good to you, what benefit is that to you? For even <u>sinners</u> do the same."*

What Christian would argue with the fact that we are to follow the example of our Savior and Lord? As we already read in 1 John 2:6: *He who says he abides in Christ ought to walk in the <u>same</u> manner <u>as He walked,</u>* and Paul said in 1 Corinthians 11:1: *Follow my example, as I follow the <u>example of Christ</u>.* But this begs the question: what did Christ <u>do</u> and what was the example He set for all those of us who claim to follow Him? We read in John 15:10: *<u>If you keep My commands,</u> you will remain in My love, <u>just as I have kept My Father's commands</u> and remain in His love.* Yes, Yeshua also walked in the anointing of the Holy Spirit to heal the sick, cast out demons and raise the dead, and He said we would do the same works He did and even greater (John 14:12), but this book focuses on living *free from sin* and living righteously (which is just as miraculous as supernatural healing and deliverance, as it is a fruit of the Spirit and not our own efforts or righteousness). Many Christians seem to have this idea that because they are saved by grace and not by their works or law-keeping, it means they don't need to aggressively deal with sin in their lives and that a *practical* and *visible* righteousness or Christlikeness is an optional pursuit (e.g., *"as long as my sin is 'covered' and 'forgiven', I'll make to heaven"*).

Many believers also confine holiness to the spiritual realm rather than the physical – focusing on the fact that we are declared "the righteousness of God in Christ", and that we are not saved by our good works, but "by grace through faith *alone.*" Amen, this is totally true! But the entire Bible, from "Genesis to maps," says that while observing God's Law can never redeem us or atone for our sin, our faith in Yeshua and our love for Him (and His love for us) *empowers* us to walk in obedience to His Word and live holy – not *for* our salvation, but *as a result* of our salvation; not out of legalistic *duty*, but out of *desire* and *love*, where keeping His commands and living holy is not a burden or religious obligation, but a joy or delight! You will hear this repeated throughout the book that God's Word makes it clear that while we are saved by grace and not works, His grace which saves us *always* produces the fruit of an obedient, godly lifestyle! We read in John 14:15, 1 John 5:3, and Titus 2:11:

"If you love Me, you <u>will</u> keep My commandments"; This is the love of God, <u>that we keep His commands</u>, and His commands are <u>not</u> burdensome; for the grace of God that brings salvation has appeared to all men, <u>instructing</u> [training] us to <u>deny ungodliness</u> and worldly lusts, and to live <u>self-controlled</u>, <u>upright</u> and <u>godly</u> lives....

If God's grace does <u>not</u> lead to a godly and obedient lifestyle, it means we have received His grace in vain (see 2 Cor.6:1; 1 Cor.15:10; Titus 2:11-12). One of the main points of this book is to help believers understand, by way of revelation, that obedience to God's commands and living in victory over sin and temptation is *not* supposed to be hard or grueling, but natural and effortless – but that can only happen as we #1, realize we are *already* clean and holy before the Lord because of His blood and our faith, and #2, *abide* in Yeshua or Christ (staying focused on Him and continually cultivating a love relationship with Him).

Is All Weakness and Carnality "Sin"?

Now that we have a biblical definition and understanding of sin, it would be helpful to make a distinction between *sin* (violating God's laws) and *weakness* (frailty and imperfections). Surely, we can say that we sin or transgress God's commands due to *weakness*, but that does not mean all weakness is confined to the "sin" of violating God's Law. If all weakness is a form of sin, remember the Lord told Paul in 2 Corinthians 12 that His power is "made perfect" in *weakness*, and Paul "boasted" about his *weaknesses* and was "content" with them so that the power of Yeshua would dwell in and upon him. Just replace the word "weakness" with "sin" in those verses and we see how it blatantly contradicts Scripture! If we read the context, Paul tells us what he is referring to when he uses the word *weaknesses* in verse 10: "insults, mistreatment, distresses, persecution, and difficulties," <u>not</u> sin or violations of God's Word.

For instance, all of us need to grow and change in areas that involve our temperament, personality, character, and behavior, but not all those areas of weaknesses are "sinful" because they do not always involve breaking God's commands. In other words, a weakness that does not involve a violation of God's Word does not make it a "sin" or make one a "sinner," even those which involve our actions. Similarly, being imperfect or flawed does not necessarily make one a "sinner." Is a godly husband a "sinner" just because he still has room for growth when it comes to serving, listening, providing, and leading as a husband, or showing more love, appreciation, and sensitivity towards his wife and children? Are godly wives "sinners" because they can show more patience and respect towards their husband or be less critical or demanding? (Excuse the stereotypes, but generally, these are the weakness of *most* husbands and wives). Also, most of us need be more disciplined with our eating habits, become better stewards of our time or be more thoughtful, thankful, and generous people; and who would not agree that we should spend more time cultivating deeper intimacy with God, sharing our faith with others or laying hands on the sick for healing, and being less focused on things in the natural realm (e.g., entertainment or time on the TV, computer, phone, Facebook, Instagram, etc.)? We can't really call such things "sin" or violations of God's commands, unless of course, the things we watch or listen to are sinful or evil.

This is important to note because many assume that because all sin springs from weakness, all weaknesses must be a form of sin. But that is not true; while most, if not all forms of weakness ultimately *come from* sin entering the world, not all weaknesses are "sinful" in that they violate God's laws (as 1 John 3:4 defines sin as transgressing God's laws). The same is true of sickness and disease; while all sickness and disease are the *ultimate result* of what theologians refer to as "original sin", which has physically marred or corrupted our DNA, personal sin is not always the direct cause of it. Having pointed this out, you can better understand how it is biblically inaccurate (to say the least) for saints or believers to call themselves "sinners" who "sin all the time."

What about the terms "carnal", "carnality", and "flesh"? Such terms always refer to *sin, evil,* or *wickedness* whenever the Bible uses them, right? In most cases, yes, but there are also times when such words simply refer to the *material, natural,* and *physical,* particularly the God-given needs and desires of our bodies, such as food, sleep, sex, etc. For example, when Paul uses the term, "carnal" he often refers to the material or physical (See Rom.15:27; 1 Cor.9:11;15:50; 2 Cor.5:16,10:3; Eph.5:29). And when Yeshua says in Matthew 26:41, *"the spirit is willing, but the 'flesh' is weak,"* the context shows He is talking about the weakness and frailty of the *physical body.* Paul also said in 1 Cor.2:14-3:2:

A <u>natural</u> man does not accept the things of the Spirit of God, for they are foolishness to him and he cannot understand them, because they are spiritually appraised (or apprehended).....but I could not speak to you as <u>spiritual</u> men, but as to men of <u>flesh</u>, as to babes in Christ. I gave you milk to drink, not solid food, for you were not able to receive it."

He was not only referring to sin, such as jealousy and strife in verse 3, but how they were still allowing their *natural* mind to dominate their lives and ways of thinking or seeing things.

Here are some examples: if we try to apprehend spiritual things or biblical truths solely with our *natural* mind and not by the Spirit of God, we are being carnal or "fleshly"; if we believe we must have an understanding or explanation for *why* God has told us to do something (in the Word or in our everyday lives) *before* we obey Him, we are being carnal; if we attempt to attain holiness and keep God's commands in the strength of our flesh and self-resolve or willpower, we are being carnal and of the flesh; if we, like "doubting Thomas," *demand* or *require* to have our *physical* senses engaged in order to have faith, we are being carnal, sensual, and fleshly[4]; if our focus, desires, passions and energy are on the things of the material realm *more* than the things of the Spirit and God's kingdom purposes, we are in fact living carnal and fleshly - even if we are living pure lives while pursuing things which are not sinful or immoral in and of themselves. This is why we are commanded *to <u>not</u> look to the things which are seen, but at the things which <u>not seen</u>; for the things which are seen are temporary, but the things which are not seen are eternal; Set your mind on things <u>above</u>, not on things that are on the earth; No one engaged in warfare <u>entangles</u> himself with the <u>everyday affairs of this life</u>, that he may please the one who enlisted him as a soldier* (2 Cor.4:18, Col.3:2, 2 Tim.2:4).

Of course, this doesn't mean we ignore and neglect the physical or that the material world is evil (as Gnosticism teaches); it simply means our focus should be on things of the spirit and fulfilling God's purposes or will, and that things of the world and material realm don't choke the Word of God in our lives and render us spiritually stagnate and unfruitful (see Matt.13:22).

What Does it Mean to "Repent"?

Now that we understand that sin and weakness are not synonymous, let us turn our attention to the terms, "repent" and "repentance." Christians who say, "once a sinner always a sinner," and that believers <u>remain</u> "sinners" even *after* conversion will quote Yeshua in Luke 5:32, *"I did not come to call the righteous, but <u>sinners</u>....."* But this is rather obvious because *who else* could He call? Were we not *all* "sinners" before we heard and answered His call? If everyone is a "sinner" before they come to Him, why did Yeshua state the obvious? As we saw in our discussion on 1 John 1:8, He said this because not everyone acknowledges they are a sinner, just as many refuse to admit they are spiritually sick, as He said in the first part of the verse, *"those who are well have no need of a physician, but those who are sick."* The Pharisees, for example, did not see themselves as "sinful" or as "sinners," which is why Yeshua's message offended them so much. But our Messiah does not just call sinners *out* of sin and the world; He calls sinners *to* something. The rest of that verse, which many omit, says He calls sinners "to <u>repentance</u>," as Yeshua said in Mark 1:15, *"The kingdom of God is at hand; <u>repent</u> and believe in the gospel."* Most of us have heard the definition of repentance is doing "a 180" or an about-face, where we make a total course correction in our life concerning our behavior. We also think repentance simply means to "stop sinning!" Of course, God desires and commands us to "stop sinning," as Yeshua said to the woman caught in adultery, *"Go your way, and <u>sin no more</u>,"* and the crippled man he healed, *"See, you are well again. <u>Stop sinning</u> or something worse may befall you."* But did you know that the Greek word for "repentance," *metanoia,* does <u>not</u> mean to change our *behavior* or *conduct?* While repentance, if genuine, always *leads* to a change in our conduct, behavior, or lifestyle, the word *metanoia* means to change our <u>mind</u> or *how we think;* it means a change in perspective or how we "see" things. ***According to Scripture, sinful thinking and behavior stem from a false perception of ourselves and our heavenly Father.***

In other words, ignorance of our true identity (e.g., an *identity crisis*) is the root cause, and as a result of this false identity and perception of God, without being aware of it, we speak and act in ways which affirm or solidify it. For example, we may say things like, *God gave up on me changing long ago – so I might as well give up on me too; I've got too many issues for God to use me or bless me; I'm only human and a 'sinner saved by grace,' so God knows I'm always going to sin and muck things up."* As Proverbs 23:7 says, *as a* *man thinks in his heart, <u>so is he</u>,* and as we read earlier in Proverbs 29:18, *where there is no vision* [or wrong vision], *the people cast off restraint.* "Casting off restraint" involves giving ourselves over to sin and becoming apathetic and accepting of it, and if we don't go that route, we can fall into the religious trap of striving to *earn* God's love and favor through the strength of our flesh, which is more offensive to God than sins of immorality (see Jer.17; Gal.3:1-7). This may explain why Paul expressed more anger towards the Galatians for their wrong *believing* than with the Corinthians for their wrong *behavior.* We may ask, *But doesn't God want us to stop sinning?* We all know that's a rhetorical question. Of course He desires and even commands us to "stop sinning" or to "sin no more," but again, our *outward* behavior is merely the fruit of our *inward* beliefs or convictions, which means merely changing our *choices* and *actions* will <u>not</u> change our *heart* or *inner* man. Yeshua made this clear in Matthew 7:18;12:33;23:26:

"A good tree cannot bear bad fruit and a bad tree cannot bear good fruit; either <u>make the tree good, and its fruit good</u>, or make the tree bad, and it fruit bad, for <u>the tree is known by its fruit</u>; Blind Pharisee, first cleanse the <u>inside</u> of the cup and dish, that the <u>outside</u> of them may be clean also."

If we are attempting to live an outwardly clean or godly life without the inside being clean, we are merely playing religion and trusting in our own efforts or performance, which therefore places us under the condemnation and judgment of the Law. We will later discuss what that means in more detail, as well as the meaning of true repentance or "changing" our mind.

CHAPTER 3

"But I'm Only Human!"

Earlier, we talked about how not all weakness is a form of sin (rooted in rebellion and unbelief). Let us touch on that topic again from a different angle. In efforts to justify habitual sin in their lives, many use the excuse, *"But I'm only human."* The implication behind this statement is that we have *no choice* but to tolerate sin and that violating God's laws and standards is *inevitable* as long as we're in these "earthen vessels." And believers will even use, or should I say *abuse*, Scripture to "support" such reasoning, with Romans 7 and 1 John 1:8 being at the top of the list. We touched on this earlier, but they will twist Yeshua's words in Matthew 26:41, where He said *the spirit is willing, but the flesh is weak.*[5] If Jesus said the flesh is "weak," then it is <u>weak</u>, right?! The flesh is indeed weak, physically, *and* spiritually, but again, the <u>context</u> clearly tells us that Yeshua was <u>not</u> talking about moral or spiritual weakness (sin), but the weakness of the *physical body* caving into its *natural* inclinations. We know this because verse 37 shows that Yeshua became angry with the disciples because they couldn't "keep watch for one hour," and kept dozing off when they should have resisted the weakness of their bodies by interceding for Him during His greatest trial. Verses 40-41 says He came to His disciples a third and fourth time, only to find them *still* sleeping because their eyes were "very heavy." Do you see how the *context* is so important? This means that because Yeshua was human like us, even *His* <u>body</u> or <u>flesh</u> was "weak" in the sense that He too became hungry, tired, or physically weary, and like any human, needed replenishment and strength through food and sleep. He even experienced emotional turmoil or weakness as He was praying in the garden of Gethsemane, asking the Father if it was possible to remove the cup of suffering He was about to drink or endure! No, it wasn't *sinful* for Him to have feelings of dread concerning what He was about to endure – that was simply a normal human emotion. If Yeshua *didn't* experience such weaknesses, that would mean He wasn't fully human, and if He wasn't fully human (yet without sin), His sacrifice would have been wasted because He wasn't truly standing in our place or acting as our true representative. [6]

It is important to note that Yeshua spoke those words of admonishment to His disciples *before* His Spirit came to *indwell* and *empower* them (and us), and <u>before </u>we could all say, "Through *Christ* I can do <u>all</u> things!" Does this mean that because Yeshua lives within us, our mortal bodies are no longer subject to weakness or frailty, or that we *cannot* sin? Like I have already affirmed several times, of course not! But to justify and tolerate moral weakness and sin in our lives by saying we are "only human" is not only unbiblical, but it also *contradicts* Scripture and is *demonic* in nature. All of us, on some level, have unknowingly embraced teachings that are unscriptural or even inspired by the enemy. But concerning this particular teaching, most of us are very familiar with 2 Corinthians 5:17: *if any man be in Christ, he is a <u>new creation</u>; old things have passed away; behold <u>all things</u> have become <u>new</u>.* According to Paul, we are <u>not</u> "only" human or mere mortals, as he admonished or *scolded* the Corinthian believers for behaving like "ordinary" or "mere" men (1 Cor.3:3). He did this because they were leading carnal or fleshly (sinful) lives, *while professing Christ as Lord and Savior*, which is obviously contrary to what Yeshua (and Paul) taught and modeled. This is why Paul could say to the Corinthians, *"we beg you on behalf of Christ, <u>be reconciled to God</u>"* (5:20). Only those who are unsaved or unregenerate need to be reconciled to God, which means this admonition only applied to believers in Corinth who had "received God's grace in vain" (6:1). Clearly, not everyone in the Church is truly born-again or truly *possesses* the faith they *profess* to have, and not all "members" of the Body of Messiah are true members (Jer.4:22; Is.29:13; Luke 13:26-27; Titus 1:16).

What does it mean to receive God's grace "in vain"? It means His grace did not bring about its intended purpose, which is to not only free us from sin, but to inspire and empower us to practically manifest or flesh-out the righteousness of God in our daily lives. If the Lord's grace does not ever-increasingly *transform, compel,* and *empower* us to effortlessly reflect the image and likeness of Yeshua, we have "received His grace in vain." As we saw earlier, God's grace toward Paul did not prove to be vain or without effect but empowered him to labor and accomplish more than the other apostles (1 Cor.15:10). We also saw that Peter tells us that we partake of Yahweh's nature, and Hebrews 12 says we *share* in His holiness. But there are still millions of believers claiming they are saved, forgiven, "cleansed and washed by the blood," and "under grace, not law," while simultaneously claiming their hearts are *wicked* and that they are *rotten sinners* who "sin all the time" in some form or another!

But again, that kind of thinking is blatantly unscriptural and even demonic, and requires a twisting of Scripture to support it. When Yahweh says we share in His divine nature and calls us a <u>royal priesthood</u> and <u>holy</u> nation, He <u>meant</u> it – not just doctrinally, spiritually, or positionally, but *physically* and *practically!* Remember, you were *predestined* to be conformed to the image of your elder brother Yeshua, and the "I AM" who stands outside of time and space, declares the end from the beginning and calls those things which are not *as though they were* - meaning He sees the finished product, which is Christ formed and manifested in *you,* the hope of glory! (See Ex.3:14; John 8:58; I1 Pet.3:8; Ps.90:2,4, 93:2, 102:12, 24-27; Is.46:10, 57:15; Rom.8:29, 4:17; Col.1:27). When He put His Spirit within you when you came into the Faith, it was His HOLY Spirit, who is given *to those who OBEY Him* (Acts 5:32). When 2 Corinthians 5:21 says we <u>are</u> the righteousness of God in Christ, that is not a religious platitude or something reserved for another day and time; it is every bit true for the *physical* and *practical* as it is for the spiritual, doctrinal, and positional!! When Yeshua said in John 8:32, *"He who the Son sets free is free indeed,"* the word "indeed" means it's *really* true that we are FREE! But what exactly is this freedom? I will address this in more detail later.

"But what about Paul?" is a common response many Christian have when they hear something that conflicts with what they've been taught concerning his writings. For instance, we read in Romans 11:32: *For God has <u>shut up all in disobedience</u> that He might show mercy to all,* and in Galatians 3:22: *But the Scripture has <u>shut up all men under sin</u> that the promise by faith in Jesus Christ might be given to those who believe.* Romans 5:20 also says: *And the Law came <u>so that the transgression</u> [sin] <u>might increase</u>; but where sin increased, grace abounded all the more.* Is Paul suggesting the blasphemous idea that Yahweh gave us His laws so that we would violate them and sin more frequently? If we read his letters in context, along with the rest of the New Testament, we can say "absolutely not!" Paul is saying the Law was given so that we not only become *aware* of our spiritually lost and dead state, but how that renders us incapable of redeeming and sanctifying ourselves through keeping His Law; He gave the Law to open our eyes to our fallen state and the heinous nature of sin, along with its destructive consequences. **God did <u>not</u> give us His Law as a means of helping us overcome sin; He gave it to help us see how sin has overcome <u>us</u> (in our unredeemed or lost state).** Religious or self-righteous people will hate that statement because they believe we can't be righteous or holy without it keeping us in check, but it's true. We read in Romans 3:20 and 7:13:

Through the Law comes knowledge [awareness] of sin; Did that which is good [the Law] bring death to me? By no means! It was sin, working death in me <u>through</u> what is <u>good</u>, in order that sin might be shown to be sin, and <u>through</u> the commandment might become sinful beyond measure.

Paul knew some of his readers would make the absurd conclusion that because grace abounds where there is sin, we can *keep sinning* or *remain a sinner* in order that God's grace may be highlighted even more, saying, *"Let us do evil that good may come out of it!"* (Rom.3:8) He addresses this in Romans 6:1-2:

What shall we say then, shall we continue in sin so that grace might increase? May it never be! How shall we died to sin live in it any longer?

But how are we to understand these verses from Romans 11 and Galatians 3? What does it mean that God and/or Scripture "shut up all mankind under sin"? It sounds like the Lord *wanted* us to fall into sin and disobedience, which He commands us <u>not</u> to do, just so that He could glorify Himself by showing us such great mercy and grace! By the way, some Christians actually believe that! This delves into the broad and often controversial topic of how God's sovereignty and our free will relate to one another (particularly through the doctrines of Calvinism and Arminianism). This topic has been hotly debated for centuries within the Church and has sadly brought about division and discord among believers. Many books have been written on this subject, but we'll briefly touch on it here. First, when Paul says God or Scripture has "shut up all" under sin and disobedience, it sounds like it means He *desires* that we sin or that He *causes* us to sin or transgress His will or laws. We read verses like Romans 9:17-18:

For the Scripture says to Pharoah, "For this very purpose I raised you up, to demonstrate My power in you, that My Name might be proclaimed throughout the whole earth. So then, He has mercy on whom He desires, and He hardens whom He desires," and God told Moses in Exodus 4:21, *"...but I will harden his* [Pharoah's] *heart so that he will not let the people go."*

Does this mean the Lord is glorified through sin and evil or that He *coerces* us to go <u>against</u> His will?[7] And if so, how can He hold us accountable, as Paul continues in Romans 9:18, *you will say to me then, "Why does He still find fault, for who can resist His will?"* Without digging too deeply into the questions and objections surrounding this topic, we need to understand that the Scriptures make it emphatically clear that because Yahweh is perfectly holy, righteous, and good, He *hates* sin or disobedience, which are rooted in pride, rebellion, and unbelief. We also read in James 1:13:

Let no one say when he is tempted, "I am being tempted by God," for God cannot be tempted by evil and <u>He Himself does not tempt anyone</u>.

Truly, it would be evil for our heavenly Father and Creator to tempt or pressure us to sin or rebel, for that is precisely *Satan's* job description and desire. It would be the greatest understatement to say that Yahweh and Satan are NOT a team working to accomplish the same goal or objective! While Yahweh certainly *tests* us for the purpose of maturing us and helping us apply what He is teaching us, He never *tempts* us or sets us up to sin or fail. Not only would it be evil for Him to tempt us to sin, as that would imply He *wants* us to sin or to disobey and rebel, but it would oppose and contradict His very nature and Word. Can you imagine Satan trying to coerce or tempt us to *obey* the Lord or to do that which is holy or righteous? Of course not, because it goes against his very nature! God tempting us to sin and rebel against Him would be no different than Him lying to us, which He *cannot* and will *never* do!

Yes, there are some things even GOD *cannot* do: Can He lie or speak falsehood? Can He be unfaithful or violate His covenant and Word? Can He be unjust and contradict Himself by coercing us to do something He commanded us *not* to do (or vice versa), and then judge us for it? If He cannot do these things because they contradict His nature, how could He be the Author of sin and evil? You may be familiar with Isaiah 45:7, where God says He *forms light and darkness, making peace and creating <u>evil</u>,* but the context shows this term refers <u>not</u> to *moral* or *ethical* evil, sin, or wickedness, but evil in the sense of disaster, calamity, grief, affliction, or distress. We shouldn't read this to mean Yahweh sovereignly orchestrates <u>all</u> painful events in our lives – anymore than we should believe people who die at a young age die because He said He "kills and makes alive" or because His Word says it is "appointed once for man to die" (Deut.32:29; Heb.9:27). It is important to note that Romans 8:28, which we quote in times of pain and loss, does <u>not</u> say God *causes all things,* period; it says He causes all things <u>to work together for good</u>. Nor does it say God causes all things to work together for good, period. It says He causes all things to work together for good – *to those who love God and who are called according to His purpose.* In other words, those who don't truly love God and are not living according to His will and purpose cannot claim that verse. Likewise, Ephesians 1:11 does <u>not</u> say God *works all things,* period; it says He works all things <u>after the counsel of His will</u>, meaning that in His infinite wisdom and power, He will see to it that His sovereign will and purpose to bring Him glory through His people <u>will</u> be accomplished (v.12). Of course, Yeshua's life is the perfect example of how our heavenly Father sovereignly uses pain and evil to accomplish His ultimate purposes in our lives. The life of Joseph is another great example. As he stepped into the fulness of his destiny, Joseph said to his brothers, the very ones who severely beat him and threw him into a well, *"You meant it for evil, BUT GOD meant it for good, in order to bring about the present result of preserving many lives."*

I just opened a can of worms with a topic that would require a separate book to do it justice, so let us get back to the main question: what does it mean when Paul says God or Scripture has "shut up all" under sin and disobedience so that He might show mercy to all? If we are going to understand Paul accurately, we must allow Scripture to interpret itself and read verses in their context. First, while it is true that literally *all* humans have been disobedient and have rebelled against God, it is not true that when it comes to *salvation* or *redemption*, the Lord shows mercy and grace to "all" people (See Rom.9:18-25; Jer.13:14, 21:7; Jos.11:20; Is.9:17, 27:11, 47:6). He certainly *offers* mercy and grace to all people, but when Paul says God "shows" mercy to "all," it should be evident that he means all *who call upon* God or all *who respond in faith to His call to surrender to Yeshua.* If all people have literally received God's mercy and grace in that their salvation is automatic (which Universalism teaches), then Yeshua was wrong when He said that *many* will enter by the gate which is wide and the road which is broad that leads to destruction. Secondly, God "shut up" all of humanity under sin not in the sense that He *makes or coerces* people sin or that He wants them to remain spiritually lost and blind, but that He "gives them over" to the desire of their hearts, allowing them to experience the full consequences of living under *the law of sin and death* (Rom.1:24,7:25,8:2). God did this to open our eyes to our plight and to condition and prepare our heart to receive our only remedy, His Son. Apart from Yeshua, or until we come new creations in Him, every human is held captive to sin, falls short of His glory, and not *one* is righteous or flawless in His sight (Rom.3:10,23). Romans 3:19-20 says:

Now we know that whatever the law says, it says to those who are under the law, so that every mouth may be silenced and the whole world held accountable to God. For by works of the law, no man will be justified in His sight, for through the law comes knowledge of sin.

If God "hardens" a person's heart, as with Pharoah, He is not giving them a renewed or "fresh" desire to sin against Him; if a person is lost, unsaved, or unregenerate, the desire or inclination to resist God and rebel against His commands is there by *default*. He simply *gives them over* to their desire to sin and their refusal to repent, allowing them to *continue* in their natural course of rebellion (Rom.1:26, 11:23; II Thess.2:11). In other words, the lost soul is "obligated" to sin and rebel, <u>not</u> because God willed it, but because that is its *natural* desire or propensity in its spiritually dead and lost state. Until we are born-again and have been given a new heart or new nature, we cannot *truly* love God and live according to His commands.

But doesn't God "allow" <u>all</u> of us to sin or do as we please? Yes, but if it is "natural" or a "given" for us to *desire* sin or to rebel against God and His ways, that is a clear sign that we are <u>not</u> born-again. One may object: *"How can you say that? Whether we are saved or not, we ALL <u>naturally desire</u> to sin!"* Such a statement shows that we believe every sinful or evil thought and desire we have (as believers) originates with *us* and that it is not an external enticement from the enemy, as we discussed a moment ago. The purpose of this book is to prove, through Scripture, that IF we are truly born-again and share God's divine nature, the "natural" desire to sin and rebel that we had before our conversion is eradicated or permanently "killed" through our co-crucifixion with Yeshua! This is not a judgment of my own; GOD emphatically says this through the writings of Paul, as we saw earlier in Romans 6:6-7. We also read in Romans 8,

Those who are dominated by the sinful nature think about sinful things, but those who are controlled by the Holy Spirit think about things that please the Spirit....the sinful nature is <u>always</u> hostile to God; it <u>never</u> did obey God's laws and it never will; that is why those who are still under the control of their sinful nature <u>can never please God</u>. But you [born-again believers] are <u>not</u> controlled by the sinful nature; <u>you are controlled by the Spirit</u> IF you have the Spirit of God living in you – and those who do not have the Spirit of Christ living in them <u>do not belong to Him at all</u>.......therefore, brothers, we are NOT under obligation to the flesh, to live according to the flesh, for if you live by its dictates, you will die, but if through the power of the Spirit you put to death the deeds of the sinful nature, you will live. For all who are led by the Spirit of God are children of God. NLT.

This begs the question we already asked in the last chapter, *"But why do I still have the desire to sin sometimes?"* It all goes back to a renewing of the mind or coming into a deeper revelation of our identity and union with the Lord. And remember, not every thought you have is your own – and the *desire* you may have at times to commit sin does <u>not</u> mean you are still a "sinner"; it simply means the patterns of the "old man" are trying to hold sway over you so that you "return to Egypt" to live as a slave again *while you are a free man!* It's <u>not</u> that the sin nature or "old man" resurrects itself, as many have been taught, but that the Enemy tries to pull us back into its *patterns* or *habits*. Not <u>one</u> verse of Scripture supports the idea that the sin nature "resurrects itself." God meant it when He said the body of sin was KILLED or CRUCIFIED (Rom.6:6), but we wrongly assume that because we are still able to sin or even have the desire to do so, it must mean our sin nature is still alive and active. We will talk more about this later, but due to false doctrines and their failure to renew their mind and stand strong in the Lord's armor, many Christians are not only living far below their birthright, but are still sitting in the prison cell with the door wide open! Who would intentionally stay in a prison with the door open? Those who were told or led to believe they still *can't* leave because sin is something they have to struggle with all their lives. Again, God said His people *perish* for <u>lack</u> of *knowledge,* and the only way we can access and walk in the freedom He provides is through knowing the TRUT (John 8:32). This surely does <u>not</u> mean we don't truly know the Lord or that we aren't saved if we're struggling due to false doctrine. When God says we "perish," that isn't confined to spiritual death; it means ignorance "destroys" our lives on many levels, sometimes to the point that we lose our physical lives.

CHAPTER 4

Romans 7 and the Apostle Paul: "Chief of Sinners"

Jesus Christ came into the world to save sinners, of whom I am chief; For we know that the Law is spiritual, but I am of the flesh, sold as a slave to sin.
1 Tim.1:15; Rom.7:14;

At the beginning at this book, I referred to 1 Timothy 4:1, where the Holy Spirit said that in the last days, many will "depart from the faith, giving heed to *deceiving spirits* and *doctrines of demons.*" Paul addresses two demonic lies in verse 3, but as God matures His Bride, He continues to reveal other damaging lies the Enemy has created and spread throughout the church, many of which were mentioned in the first chapter. Here are two we will address now:

We cannot help but sin, because until we leave these "fleshly tents" behind, we'll always be fighting to overcome the evil desires of our sinful nature.

The more aware we become of our sinful and depraved nature, the more spiritually mature we are.

Perhaps you have believed these lies yourself – or maybe you *still* believe they reflect biblical truth. For many years of my Christian walk, I believed these lies myself and even taught them to others. Sure, many Christians pull verses out of the Bible and use them to support such beliefs, but this book will show that their conclusions are the result of not "rightly dividing the Word" or "accurately handling the Word of truth" (2 Tim.2:15). If you believe such statements define a born-again, Spirit-filled believer, please continue reading and remember the disclaimer that this book does <u>not</u> promote the doctrine of Perfectionism – the belief that not only has our sin nature been crucified or "killed" through our union with Christ (which *is* biblical), but that true believers *cannot* and *will never* sin or violate God's Word simply because the "Holy" Spirit indwells them (or that if they do sin, they must not be born-again). But the idea that a believer cannot or will never sin is no less false and unbiblical than saying they will *remain* "sinners" who *always* sin and *struggle to overcome it until they die.* The key words are "always" and "struggle"; if we are *always* (routinely and habitually) sinning or breaking God's commands and grieving His Spirit, and if overcoming sin is a constant *struggle* or *battle,* we can all agree that is <u>not</u> God's will for His children. The problem is that they would also say "that's just the way it is this side of glory," or something along those lines. One of the most common passages used to defend the belief that Christians will always have to fight or struggle to overcome their sinful nature is Romans chapter seven, where Paul describes the misery of living with two equally opposing desires within us – one desire to *observe* God's laws, with an opposing desire and inclination to *violate* His laws. Paul describes this in verses 15-17,25:

For that which I am doing, I do not understand; for I am not practicing what I would like to do [keep God's laws]*, but I am doing the very thing that I hate* [breaking God's laws]*. But if I do the very thing I do not wish to do, I agree with the Law, confessing that it is good. So now, no longer am I the one doing it* [breaking God's laws]*, but sin which indwells me....So then, on the one hand I myself with my mind am serving the Law of God, but on the other, with my flesh the law of sin.*

The assumption is made that because Paul is using 1st person language in this chapter, it means he must be talking about *himself* and/or describing his *present, personal* experience *as a born-again believer* in Christ. The same applies to 1 Timothy 1:15, where he describes himself, with present tense language, as the "chief of sinners." But the basics of Hermeneutics (the rules of correctly interpreting Scripture) tell us how important it is to consider the *context* in question. If we read the context of Romans seven, keeping in mind the entire letter of Romans and the rest of Paul's letters on this subject, we will see he is simply utilizing 1st person language to get his point across (just as he often used hyperbole or exaggeration). [8]

Even if Paul *was* literally talking about himself, we know he was <u>not</u> referring to his *present* or *current* experience as a believer, but about his life *before* his conversion. Just as Jeremiah 17:9 refers to the state of <u>lost</u> humanity when it says, "the heart is deceitful and desperately sick," so Paul, using 1st person language, refers to the condition and dilemma of humanity as a whole – in their spiritually *dead* and *unregenerate* state. This is not speculation, as he writes in Romans 7:14, *we know that the Law is spiritual, but I am <u>unspiritual</u>, sold as a <u>slave</u> to sin.* Really? Paul, who is often hailed as the godliest, Spirit-filled believer who ever lived, was "unspiritual" and a "slave to sin"? If he really was unspiritual, or saw himself that way, he would have been a hypocrite for scolding other believers for being *unspiritual* or behaving as "mere men" (I Cor.3:1-3).

Paul was <u>not</u> a hypocrite because he wrote and preached extensively and passionately about being *freed* or *liberated* from the dominion of sin and the sin nature itself. But it is wrong to put Paul on a pedestal like we have - as we do with many other people or ministers. Surely he was a great model to follow, as he even encourages us to follow his example because he was following the example of Christ (I Cor.11:1; Phil.3:17). But if we are one with Yeshua, we have access to *everything* Paul and every other "great" Christian throughout history had. Like him, <u>no one</u> who is united with Yeshua and indwelt by the "Holy" Spirit of God can be "sold" under sin and a "slave" to it! The sin nature and sin-consciousness that we inherited from Adam *no longer* has dominion over us as believers – where we are still in its clutches and "cannot help" but sin and rebel against our Savior and God! If we are being honest, the reason Romans seven is used to justify the belief that even *born-again believers* are weak and depraved "sinners" (albeit forgiven) who are bound to struggle with sin until we physically die, is to make *excuses* for our sin, ungodly attitudes, and behaviors that we call "weaknesses" that stem from our "mere" humanity! Again, the Bible makes it crystal clear, especially *Paul*, that we as believers are NOT slaves to sin and that it no longer controls us or holds sway over us; we are no longer slaves of sin and our flesh because Christ has made us <u>masters</u> over them. If we cannot be free from sin's grip until we die and reach the "sweet by and by," how would that not ultimately make <u>death</u> our "savior," rather than Yeshua?! When Paul said in Romans 6:7 that *he who has died is freed from sin,* he isn't saying we will be free from sin once we physically die – he's saying all throughout that chapter that if we are born-again and have been joined to Christ, we <u>already</u> died *with* Him on the cross, and are therefore are NOW free from sin (verses 2,6-8,11,18)!

But Paul said He "Died Daily" to Sin!

Many Christians, including pastors and theologians, believe Paul indeed battled with resisting and overcoming sin and temptation because he said he was the "chief of sinners" who apparently "died daily" (1 Cor.15:31). The inference and assumption is that Paul is talking about dying daily to *sin,* yet he makes <u>no</u> mention of sin in the context of this statement. This is another shining example of lazy and irresponsible Bible study (or *butchering*)! Again, if we just read the context – which is so easy to do, we'll see what Paul is saying. Look at what Paul says right <u>before</u> the popular verse, "I die daily," which many Christians pluck out of context: *We are in danger every hour. I affirm, by the boasting in you which I have in Christ, I die daily.*

Then the verse right <u>after</u> he mentions "danger" and "dying daily," he says: *what do I gain, if <u>humanly</u> speaking, I fought with wild beasts at Ephesus?* How is it not clear that when Paul said he died daily, he was saying that in his efforts to spread the gospel, his life was literally or physically hanging in the balance at every turn as he contended with those who were antagonistic towards the gospel message and the Lord's followers? Not *one* comment is made about sin or a sin nature! If we just read chapter fifteen of the same letter, we see that Paul's topic is not about sin or dying to it, but about *physical* death and resurrection, and how the first Adam brought condemnation and death to all mankind through his disobedience or sin, while Yeshua, the last Adam, brought us atonement, life, and salvation through His obedience and righteousness. Paul goes into more detail about the physical dangers of spreading the gospel in 2 Corinthians 11:23-33, and uses similar language in 4:11 and 6:4-9,

For we who live are <u>always delivered unto death</u> for Jesus' sake, that the life of Jesus may also be manifested in our mortal flesh; so then, <u>death works in us</u>, but life in you; .....in everything we commend ourselves as servants of God, in much endurance, afflictions, hardships, distresses, beating, imprisonments, tumults, labors, sleeplessness, hunger....as unknown yet well-known, as <u>dying</u>, yet behold, we live, as punished, <u>yet not put to death.</u>

But for argument's sake, let's assume Paul was in fact talking about "dying to sin" every day. The irony is that those who believe this do not truly apply that interpretation to their walk of faith. If Paul was saying he died to SIN daily, it means he did just that – *he died to sin or his sin nature daily or constantly!* That would mean that moment by moment, he *refused* to give in to sin and temptation, and *consistently* chose to walk in godliness, righteousness, and obedience to God's commands. If we mean "dying to sin daily" is living with a constant reminder and awareness that we *already* died to sin by our union with Yeshua, then there is nothing wrong with using that terminology (even though that isn't what Paul was saying here). It would be more biblically accurate to say, "Through Christ, I <u>AM</u> DEAD to sin" and "I <u>HAVE</u> DIED to sin," (present and past tense) as Romans 6:11 and Colossian 3:3-5 emphatically say. However, when most Christians say they die to sin daily, what they mean is this: they <u>expect</u> that "dying to sin" is a perpetual *fight* or *struggle*, where they wake up every day saying to themselves with gritted teeth and clinched fists, "I *must not* sin today; I *will not* sin today!" And Romans seven is a key passage that is grossly misinterpreted and misused to feed that lie and mentality. Some may ask, "What's wrong with starting our day like that?" What's wrong with such thinking is that it not only causes us to rely on self-resolve or willpower to overcome sin and temptation, but totally undermines and even denies the truth that our Lord and Savior already took care of the sin problem and that by our union with Him, we are ALREADY dead to it! Even if we say we're "trying" to resist sin in the *Lord's* strength and not our own, that suggests He didn't *already* set us free – not only from the penalty and consequence of sin, but from the sin nature altogether! If we are constantly struggling or fighting to overcome sin and yet find ourselves sinning "all the time" or "everyday" as many believers confess, Paul clearly gives us the solution to such a dilemma in Romans 7:24-25a (remember he is speaking on behalf of those who remain under the dominion of sin or those who are still unregenerate):

Wretched man that I am, who will <u>rescue</u> me from this body of death? Thanks be to God through Jesus Christ our Lord!

The truth is, if we have become one spirit with Yeshua, share in His divine nature, and it is no longer us living but HE who lives in us, we simply need to pray for the revelation that we have *already* been rescued or *set free* from the body of sin and that our old carnal nature (that loved sin and was held captive by it) <u>is</u> *already* crucified or dead! We need to pray for a greater revelation of the truth that our old carnal nature was *already* conquered by the <u>finished</u> work of Yeshua - <u>not</u> by our self-resolve or willpower (more on this later). If we're asking the Lord to help and rescue us from sin or temptation, I can imagine Him saying: *"I've <u>already</u> done it! My work is FINISHED! Your part is to just to BELIEVE that it's done and to abide in ME – when you do that, sin and temptation will become for you what I've <u>already</u> made it: a <u>non-issue</u>!"* Doesn't Paul clearly say that he who <u>has</u> died is *freed* or acquitted from sin, which is why we can "consider" or reckon ourselves <u>dead</u> to it?

For the law of the Spirit of life in Christ Jesus has <u>set you free</u> from the law of sin and death! (Rom.6:7,11; 8:2).

Again, many will object: *"Yeah, BUT our old man daily 'resurrects' itself and therefore must be 'daily crucified!'"* As noted, other than the fact that the Bible never says anything like that, how much sense does that make? If something has been truly crucified or killed, how you can't possibly kill it again, let alone countless more times! And here's the most important question: ***How can we truly "consider ourselves" DEAD to sin, as Romans 6:11 commands us, while maintaining the confession and conviction that we are "sinners" who "sin all the time," and have no choice but to contend with it daily?*** Let's be honest, this doctrine was concocted in efforts to justify or make room for sin and the constant struggle or battle with sin and temptation that many of us have known. In other words, we have interpreted Scripture through the lens of our experience (or lack thereof), rather than allowing the Word to truly speak for itself. This may not have been done with the intention to embrace sin, but such false doctrines produce the <u>rotten *fruit*</u> of captivity to sin, or at best, a life of "sin-management." But Yeshua didn't lay down His life for us so that we can "manage" sin – He gave His life so that we might be totally FREED from it! But as they say, "Garbage in, garbage out," and Proverbs 23:7, a verse often quoted in this book, says: *As a man thinks in his heart, so IS he.*

The second half of Romans 7:25 says, *So then, with my mind I myself am serving the law of God, but with my flesh, the law of sin.* Many will stop right there and say, "See – Paul says that even though we have the *desire* to keep God's laws, our flesh serves the law of sin." But remember, Paul is speaking on behalf of *unregenerate* people, <u>not</u> born-again new creations in Christ! They go a step further in butchering this passage by adding the next verse, which says *there is no condemnation for those are in Christ* (8:1). Amen - there is indeed NO condemnation, guilt, or shame if we are joined to our Savior, but the implication is that because of this, many believe they can *tolerate* sin or even "snuggle up" to it as though it isn't a huge deal – especially when they see themselves as "only human." They reason: "If the 'great saint and apostle Paul' battled with sin and temptation, who am I to think *I* won't?" Even if someone like Paul truly struggled with sin and temptation, why would we have to assume we are also doomed to live that way? Paul was indeed a very mature and spiritual man, but like everyone else, he was daily maturing in his walk with God. He even admitted at the end of his life that he had not yet "arrived" and was still "pressing on toward the goal" (Phil.2:12-14). Anyhow, the conclusion many draw is that because we are under grace and because God does not condemn us for our sin if we are in Christ, it means we can accommodate it, tolerate it, or not be too concerned if we still routinely commit it or struggle with it. But look at what Hebrews 10:26-30 says:

For if we go on sinning willfully after receiving the knowledge of the truth, there no longer remains a sacrifice for sins, but a certain terrifying expectation of judgment and the fury of fire which will consume the adversaries. Anyone who sets aside the Law of Moses dies without mercy on the testimony of two or three witnesses. How much severer punishment do you think he will deserve who has trampled underfoot the Son of God, and has regarded as unclean the blood of the covenant by which he was sanctified, and has insulted the spirit of grace? For we know Him who said, "Vengeance is Mine, I will repay." And again, "The Lord will judge His people. It is a terrifying thing to fall into the hands of the living God.

Some may say, *"Believers are not God's "adversaries" or enemies – so those verses are not talking about Christians."* Of course, true believers are not Yahweh's enemies, but these verses are addressing those who have "received the *knowledge* of truth." This means he is clearly talking about those who *intellectually* "know" and even believe the truth of God in Christ, but whose deeds deny Him or whose life holds to a form of godliness but denies its power to transform them into the likeness of Yeshua. We *know* the church is filled with those who turn the grace of God into licentiousness or use it as an excuse to live in sin (Titus 1:16; 2 Tim.3:5; Jude 1:4; Acts 20:29-30). It is important to note that the author is clearly <u>not</u> using what many would call "Old Covenant" language when speaking about judgment and vengeance because he is writing *after* Yeshua's sacrifice. The New Testament makes it clear that if a so-called Christian is *living* in sin and seeks to justify habitual sin in their lives, they stand before God as an *ungodly* and *condemned* person who, by their lifestyle, *deny* our Lord Yeshua. This is not speculation, as Jude 1:4 and Titus 1:16 clearly say:

For certain men have crept in unnoticed, those who were long beforehand marked out for this <u>condemnation,</u> <u>ungodly</u> persons who <u>turn the grace of our God into licentiousness</u> and <u>deny</u> our only Master and Lord, Jesus Christ;

They <u>profess</u> to know God, but <u>by their deeds</u> they <u>deny</u> Him, being detestable and disobedient, worthless for any good deed.

Remember, if we are a true believer, Romans 6:6-8 says:

....our old self WAS crucified <u>with</u> Him, that our body of sin might be <u>done away with</u>, that we should <u>no longer</u> be slaves to sin; for he who HAS died is FREED from sin. Now if we HAVE DIED with Christ [to sin], *we believe we shall also live with Him* [to righteousness].

But Didn't Jesus Say we are to 'Take up our Cross'?

Indeed, Yeshua said in Matthew 16:24, *"If anyone shall come after Me, he must <u>deny</u> himself, <u>take up his cross</u> and follow Me."* Most of us have been taught this means we are to constantly do our best to "die to sin," as Paul supposedly said he did. But as we just saw, chapters 6-8 of Romans make it abundantly clear that if we are joined to Yeshua, we are to consider ourselves ALREADY dead to sin – <u>not</u> that we *keep* "dying" to it or crucifying it every day. If our sin nature needs to be constantly crucified, that clearly implies it constantly "resurrects" itself, which in turn implies our Lord's sacrifice did not get the job done, even though He said "it is finished!" Besides the fact that not even *one* verse of Scripture supports this view, as already noted - it is utter nonsense! Apart from the physical or bodily resurrection of the dead, if our old, spiritually dead self was truly crucified or killed, how could it "resurrect" *itself?* Granted, it *can* be difficult to resist sin and temptation at times, but the degree of difficulty depends on the level of revelation we are walking in concerning our true identity in the Lord. This is why we must constantly pray for greater revelation of what it practically means to be crucified with Yeshua, where His death to sin "once for all" means we too died to sin "once for all" by our union with Him. Do dead people sin? As we have already seen in Romans 6:7, Paul says they do <u>not</u>: *For he who <u>has died</u> is <u>freed</u> from sin.* Of course, *physically* dead people don't sin and are *unable* to violate God's Law, but the context shows Paul is talking about *spiritual* death to sin or *spiritual* freedom from sin. But if Yeshua does not sin because He is dead to it, and we are one spirit with Him, then it stands to reason (and especially Scripture) that we should not sin either! Yes, we know Yeshua <u>never</u> committed sin or was *never* "alive" to it, but if we have been born-again, we are a brand-new creation in Him - a new creature or species, if you will. Paul goes on to say in verses 10-11:

.....for the death He died, He died to sin <u>once and for all</u>, but the life He lives, He lives to God. Even so, <u>consider yourselves to be dead to sin</u>, but alive to God in Christ Jesus.

Here is an important question: Who's cross was Jesus carrying and on who's cross was He crucified: was it *His* cross, or *our* cross? If we get to carry our own cross, then who's cross did Yeshua die upon? Do not misunderstand, Yeshua <u>did</u> have a cross of His own to bear, but it was one that <u>no one</u> could carry but HIM – not only the cross of willingly laying down His life to atone for our sins and cleanse our consciences, but to restore our relationship with Him <u>and</u> restore us back to His image and likeness. His cross was obviously <u>not</u> one of denying a sin nature and having to kill or crucify His flesh or the "old man." His cross had nothing to do with HIS sin because He is sinless, and everything to do with OUR sin, as 1 Peter 2:24 says:

"He bore <u>our</u> sins in His body, so that, having died to sins, we might live for righteousness, for by His wounds you <u>were</u> healed."

So ultimately, Yeshua's cross was <u>not</u> His, because it would be a gross understatement to say He did nothing to deserve it – as the Scriptures clearly say He was and will forever be the *perfect* reflection, manifestation or embodiment of the Father's nature, essence and being. So, when Yeshua tells us to "take up our cross daily," He is *not* telling us to crucify our sin nature, not only because that already occurred by our union with His death, but because *killing* the old man (not simply bruising him) and eradicating sin was the whole point of His death - something we could *never* do! Besides the fact that self-crucifixion is impossible, if we <u>could</u> crucify our sin nature and sanctify ourselves, what would be the point of Yeshua's sacrifice?

If we could obtain righteousness on our own or make ourselves perfect or right before the Lord through SELF-denial and SELF-resolve, Galatians 2:21 says His sacrifice would have been a waste!

When Yeshua says we are to deny ourselves and take up our cross, He's telling us to do the opposite of what we have been taught: When we consider the whole counsel of Scripture on this topic, we will understand He is saying that if we want to be His disciple and find true life, we must fully relinquish all self-trust, along with our "right" to be the captain of our own destiny, where we chart our *own* course and live as though <u>we</u> are what life is all about. As Yeshua said *"for whoever wishes to save his life shall lose it, but whoever <u>loses his life</u> for My sake shall <u>find</u> it"* (Matt. 16:25). Our Lord is the perfect example of fully surrendering our lives to the Father, as He said of Himself, *"For I have come down from heaven <u>not</u> to do My own will, but the will of Him who sent Me."* And we can never forget His words He prayed just before His crucifixion, *"not My will, but THY will be done."*[9] Losing our lives does <u>not</u> mean we disdain our lives[10] or that we lose our freedom and responsibility to make good or wise decisions; it means we die to our own will and surrender our own ambitions and dreams to Him and seek to fulfill HIS will for our lives and seek HIS kingdom above all things. Jeremiah 29:11, one of our favorite verses, does <u>not</u> say the Lord knows the plans YOU have for yourself, but that He knows the plans HE has for you. Now of course, this doesn't mean we can't make plans or have goals and dreams we want to fulfill. If you know the Bible, you will know that when we fully surrender our life to His Lordship, and we find our identity, fulfillment, and joy in Him alone, He will grant us the desires of *our* hearts (Ps.37:4; John.15:7). The reason for this is because when we are truly surrendered to Him, our desires will *naturally* align with that which please HIM and fulfill HIS dreams or plans for us, not things that are rooted in selfish ambition, greed, materialism, or the attempt to find our identity and value outside of Him.

More importantly, Yeshua is saying that we have to relinquish and renounce all self-effort of saving or redeeming ourselves, establishing our own righteousness, and attempts to merit or earn Yahweh's love, acceptance, favor, and blessing. He calls us to repudiate all attempts of spiritual advancement or oneness with Yahweh through self-achievement or the flesh. As Yahweh says, *"Cursed is the man who trusts in mankind and makes flesh his strength;" "Not by might, nor by power, but by My Spirit," says the Lord* (Jer.17:5; Zech.4:6). Yeshua also said the flesh profits nothing, and that apart from Him, we can DO nothing. This means any doctrine that places the focus on what *you* need to do for God, rather than what HE has done for you (single-handedly and without your help), diminishes His glory and spits on the finished work of the cross! He is telling us that just as *He* denied Himself by fully living His life to please and glorify the Father, we are to live our lives for the same purpose - not for ourselves and our own agendas and ambitions, but for HIM and His kingdom, even if that leads to great sacrifice or suffering persecution and physical death! When we read the Gospels or the New Testament in context, it is clear that our Lord isn't talking about us crucifying our sin nature (which again is impossible), but about following Him at all costs, trusting in Him alone, loving Him, and seeking His kingdom and righteousness above all else. So, when 1 John 2:6 tells us to walk in the same manner He walked, that does not mean we take on a savior complex and act like we can atone for our own sins or purge ourselves of evil through self-resolve or willpower. And it certainly doesn't mean, as religion would have us believe, that we are to try to live how Jesus lived in our own strength. If we try to do that, not only will we burn-out or fall into pride, we will fall under God's curse and condemnation for attempting to save and sanctify ourselves through self-righteous religiosity.

We need to remember that the cross is a symbol that represents a curse, as Galatians 3:13 says, *For Christ redeemed us from the curse of the law, having become a curse for us, for it is written, 'cursed is everyone who is hung on a tree.'* It is important to note that Paul is NOT saying, as the Church at large says he is, that the curse we were redeemed from is God's Law *itself.* Yahweh's Law cannot possibly be a curse because it reflects His very nature! He calls it "great and glorious," and the Scriptures testify that it is perfect, changeless, and everlasting, and that observing it brings *life* and *blessing* (Is.42:21; Ps.19:7; Deut.4:2,6:2-3,32:4,28:1-14; Lev.18:5; Rom.7:12). Of course, God's Word or Law is perfect, changeless, and everlasting, as it reveals His character, and He clearly said He never changes and never alters what He has spoken (Ps.89:34; Mal.3:6)! Paul is saying we have been redeemed or released from the curse OF the Law or the curses IN God's Law which come against us for violating it. We read in Deuteronomy 11:26-28:

"See, I am setting before you today a blessing and a curse; the <u>blessing</u>, IF you listen to the commandments of the Lord your God,...and the <u>curse</u>, IF you do not listen to the commandments of the Lord your God, but turn aside from the way which I am commanding you today."

As alluded to above, the only way the Law *itself* can curse us is when we use it in a way that Yahweh did <u>not</u> intend – that is, when we trust in our observance of the Law as our source of restoration with God and our redemption, salvation, and sanctification. This topic is the heart of this book, which we will later discuss in more detail.

All of this has to do with our <u>character</u> or <u>nature</u>. Sinning is indeed *natural* for all of humanity, but if it is natural for us as *born-again believers,* where it's not only habitual or routine, but *pleasurable* and does not *grieve* us, that is a huge red flag! Yes, sin is a short-lived "pleasure" as Hebrew 11:25 says, but if we are not relying on the Lord's power and grace to walk in the victory He has already given us and we zealously give ourselves over to sin with little to no concern, then according to Scripture, we are indeed a "sinner" who is <u>not</u> born-again or spiritually regenerated and transformed. However, if sin is *heinous* and *grievous* to us, and if everything in us *desires* to glorify the Lord and *love* His commands, such fruit is a clear sign that we are indeed a "new creation" and that we are God's <u>saint</u>! As Philippians 2:13 says, as we work <u>out</u> our salvation, God works *in* us to <u>will</u> and <u>act</u> *according to His good pleasure.*

And doesn't the Holy Spirit "convict" people of sin, as Yeshua said in John 16:8? Yes, He convicts the <u>world</u> or lost <u>sinners</u> of their sin, as Jude v.15 affirms, but if you're sinning as a *believer,* God's Spirit doesn't scold or reprimand you as a "guilty convict," but reminds you that because you share His nature and are one spirit with Him in Yeshua, you are *righteous, holy* or *set apart,* and that you are <u>not</u> a sinner but a *saint* who has totally lost their appetite for sin (that is, if you truly know who you are in Him)! Yes, if you are indwelt by the Spirit of God or Yeshua, you are His *saint,* as the Scriptures testify over and over! Contrary to popular belief, a saint is not someone who lives a perfect or flawless life, as religion would have you believe, but someone who's nature has been transformed by grace to love what God loves and hate what He hates - which begs the question: What does God hate? That is a "no-brainer"- sin, right? Correct, but as noted earlier, most Christians do not know how the Bible defines sin. Again, 1 John 3:4 says: *sin is the transgression of the law* [lawlessness or living apart from His Law], and Romans 3:23 says *all have sinned and fallen short of God's glory* or "missing the mark." But why does God hate sin so much? Not only because sin shows our lack of faith or trust in God's wisdom and goodness, and especially His love for us, but because it robs us of the peace, joy, and freedom we can experience when we live according to His Word, laws, or commandments. Yes, this is Christianity 101, but many professing Christians do not understand such basics.

Let me again make it clear that I am *not* saying those of us who are truly born-again and have had our sin nature crucified with Christ are no longer <u>able</u> to sin or that we <u>never</u> sin. But there's a huge difference between <u>practicing</u> sin, where it's a *pattern* or *routine*, and <u>committing</u> sin or behaving in a manner that is inconsistent with our new nature. Of course, those who routinely sin "commit" sin, *naturally* and without any godly sorrow over it, but *committing* a sin does not necessarily make us a "sinner," any more than obeying some of God's commands makes us a righteous person or a "saint." We already touched on this, but you might object: *"But if my sin nature or my old carnal man truly IS dead or has been eradicated, then why and how do I still sin as a Christian?"* That is a great question. If we are a born-again Spirit-filled believer who has become one spirit with Christ, why and how would we desire to continue sinning or willfully violate God's laws? If it is no longer us living but *Yeshua* living in us, as Galatians 2:20 says, sin is no longer a part of our spiritual makeup or DNA! As Paul said, if any man be in Christ, he is a NEW creation or species; the old has passed away and ALL things are NEW!

First of all, the primary reason truly born-again Christians struggle with sin is because they are fully persuaded and convinced, through false doctrine, that they are still "sinners" who have no choice but to struggle with it. We will discuss this in more detail in chapter 7, but it is impossible for your outward or physical life to rise above the level of your inner thoughts and beliefs. You may do so through sheer willpower and self-resolve, but it won't last long because the "thermostat" of your beliefs and convictions will eventually bring your life back down to the true "temperature" you've set it on. How many of us have gotten excited about various New Year's resolutions we've made, only to find ourselves going right back to old habits – usually within just days? If we try to change our lives without first making changes in our hearts and minds, which impact our emotions, choices, and actions, any changes we make simply won't last. For instance, if you see yourself and speak of yourself as an "over-eater" and glutton, you'll never make permanent lifestyle changes in your diet. The same principle applies to your struggle with sin and temptation; if you believe you are a "weak sinner" or that sinning is inevitable, that's precisely what your life will manifest!

Secondly, we must understand that not every thought we have is our *own,* and the Enemy works really hard to convince us otherwise. Why? Because if he can convince us that sinful or evil thoughts, desires, and temptations originate with *us,* we will believe the lie that we are still sinful or that our hearts remain impure, depraved, and wicked. But remember, Scripture speaks of the "deceitfulness of sin," and tells us that those who belong to Christ have *crucified the flesh,* along with its passions and desires (Heb.3:13; Gal.5:24). If this is true, all sinful thoughts and temptations are *external enticements* from the Enemy, not coming from within or stemming from your true identity in Yeshua! ***If you believe all sinful thoughts and desires originate with YOU, you will not only feel guilty or condemned, you will also vainly attempt to fight against yourself to become holy or righteous - relying on the flesh to overcome or kill the flesh, which is impossible.*** Remember, you are *already* holy and righteous by your faith in Yeshua, not by your own efforts to resist sin, clean yourself up, and live right!

We also need to remember that just because our sin nature was dealt a death blow at the cross does <u>not</u> mean we are no longer free moral agents who can *choose* to obey or disobey, or to walk in wisdom and freedom <u>or</u> foolishness and bondage. In other words, we will always have the freedom and choice to act *in* or *out* of alignment with our new nature and identity in Yeshua. That is the risk involved in a love relationship. Again, taking on the new man and the nature of our Messiah does not make us puppets who have no free will. Until a person becomes one spirit with Yeshua and begins to share His nature, the old <u>sin</u> nature they inherited from Adam still dominates them, and their minds are set on the flesh, making it impossible for them to submit to God's laws *naturally,* out of a *love* and *desire* that flows from the new nature. Romans 8:5-9,12-13; Galatians 5:16 say:

For those who are according to the flesh set their minds on the things of the flesh, but those who are according to the Spirit, the things of the Spirit. For the mind set on the flesh is death, but the mind set on the Spirit is life and peace, because the mind set on the flesh is hostile towards God; for it does not subject itself to the law of God, for it is <u>not even able</u> to do so; and those who are in the flesh <u>cannot</u> please God. However, YOU are <u>not</u> in the flesh, but in the Spirit - if indeed the Spirit of Christ dwells in you, and if Christ is in you, though the body is dead because of sin, yet the spirit is alive because of righteousness. But if anyone does not have the Spirit of Christ, he does not belong to Him. So brethren, we are under obligation, <u>not</u> to the flesh, to live according to the flesh, for if you live according to the flesh, you will die, but if by the Spirit you put to death the misdeeds of the body, you will live.

But I say, walk by the Spirit, and you will <u>not</u> carry out the desire of the flesh.

Due to unbelief and a need to justify besetting sin in their life, many Christians will identify with Galatians 5:17, the very next verse: *For the flesh sets its desire against the Spirit, and the Spirit against the flesh; for these are in opposition to one another, so that you may do the things which you please.* We've already seen that Paul also spoke about this in Romans chapters seven and eight, but the very next verse, Galatians 5:18, says: *BUT, <u>IF</u> you are led by the Spirit, you are <u>not</u> under the Law,* and verse 25 says *those who belong to Yeshua <u>have crucified</u>* [past tense] *the flesh with its passions and desires.* We will later address in more detail what it means to not be "under the Law," but for now we must point out that it does <u>not</u> mean we can live however we please or that God's Law is now null and void. If Paul was saying God's laws were abolished because we are "under grace and not law," he would be contradicting himself all throughout his letters because he frequently speaks of the importance of living righteous lives, which His Law clearly reflects. It would make zero sense to say that being led by the Spirit enables us to live righteously while also saying we are no longer required to keep the Law – the very Law which *defines* righteousness. We will also discuss how not living "under the law" is the same as not living "by" the Law, and what it means to no longer be under what Paul calls the "law of sin and death." At this point, you might agree with Peter who said in 2 Peter 3:16 that some of Paul's writings are "difficult" or "hard to understand," but the fog will lift as we progress.

There is much we could discuss about the above verses from Romans and Galatians, but I will comment on three things:

1) Paul is clearly saying that if you are of the flesh (meaning the passions or desires of your flesh dominate you), that means you do not have the Spirit of Christ, and as a result, you are "held captive" by sin and "obligated" to live by the flesh – as he says in v.8-9, that you do not even have the *ability* to submit to God's Law and please Him.[11] But then he goes on to say that if you <u>do</u> have

the Spirit of Yeshua, you are *obligated* to live by His Spirit. In this context, "obligated" does not mean *have* to or *ought* to, but that because we now share His heart and nature, we "can't help" but live righteously or by His Spirit because we <u>want</u> or <u>desire</u> to do so! Just as a sinner is a *willful* slave to sin because they love and desire to commit it (and cannot fully overcome it by their own strength), so a Spirit filled believer is a *willful* slave to Yeshua and is "obligated" to live righteously because they have been transformed to truly love Him and His ways (see Romans 6:19-22). It is not that we as born-again believers can't sin or disobey if we want to; it is that God's love and grace transforms us so that we no longer *desire* to sin or tolerate it. If we are still struggling with the *desire* to sin and have difficulty resisting it, we simply need to renew our minds with the Word, cultivate a greater intimacy with the Lord, and mature in our revelation of our true identity in Him.

2) Notice how Paul speaks of putting to death the misdeeds of the BODY and <u>not</u> of the "sinful nature." Why? Because our sin nature was crucified with Yeshua, as Paul made abundantly clear in Romans chapters six and seven. This proves that ***a sinful nature is not required for us to have the ability or "freedom" to violate God's laws or to sin.*** The enemy would have us believe that if and when we commit sin with our *body,* that must mean we are still "sinners" who have to contend with a "very much alive" sin nature. But that is a LIE! Otherwise, how do you think Adam and Eve got themselves into trouble in the first place? Before heeding the voice of the enemy and choosing to disobey Yahweh or sin against Him, were they not *perfect* or <u>without</u> sin? Not only were they sinless and morally flawless, the "sin nature" or "carnal man" did not yet exist! If Adam and Eve had the ability and freedom to disobey or sin, *while in a state of perfection or sinlessness,* why wouldn't we, who previously *lived* in sin, be able to do the same in our redeemed, justified, and sanctified state? You see, the Lord cannot possibly have

an intimate relationship with us unless He protects and preserves our free will because without it, a genuine relationship based on love cannot possibly exist – as "forced love" is a contradiction in terms, and God certainly does not coerce us to choose righteousness or manipulate us to draw close to Him and pursue intimacy with Him.

3) Notice the way Galatians 5:16 is worded, which is very important. It says we will not gratify the desires of our flesh *when we walk by the Spirit*; it does <u>not</u> say we will walk by the Spirit when we do not carry out the desires of our flesh. We cannot get this backwards as the spirit of religion and a salvation-by-works mentality would have us do. ***If you try to kill or subdue the misdeeds of the body BY the body, or depend on your flesh to resist your flesh, that means you are still placing confidence in yourself (your willpower or self-resolve), and when you do that, you end up empowering and "reactivating" the patterns of the old man.*** This is the dilemma or conflict Paul was talking about in Romans 7. He clearly said that we put to death the misdeeds of the body *by the Spirit,* and that we are not to put *any* confidence in our flesh or own strength (Rom.8:13; Phil.3:3-9). We are to find our ourselves in Yeshua alone, not attempting to establish a righteousness of our own through our fleshly efforts of keeping God's laws – as our righteousness comes from GOD on the basis of faith.

If believers who lived before Yeshua came were to live by faith and not trust in their own works and strength, why would it be any different for us? (e.g., see Zech.4:6; Jer.17:5; Hab.2:4). Paul discusses in Philippians how he had every reason (before man, not God) to boast in the accomplishments of his flesh, particularly concerning his conformity to God's Law, even labeling himself "blameless." But Paul learned by revelation that the righteousness God desires from us is *not* mere outward conformity to His laws or commands. Observing God's Law *does* make us "righteous" in a practical sense, but that kind of righteousness does not transform our *nature, heart,* or *spirit* - nor does it redeem and sanctify us or make us worthy of salvation. If we could be "worthy" of salvation or merit God's love and acceptance through our obedience, Yeshua's sacrifice would be meaningless (Gal.2:21). The only righteousness God truly desires and accepts is the *inner* and *perfect spiritual* righteousness that comes only by grace through faith alone in the righteousness and perfect sacrifice of Yeshua our Messiah. And once we receive this righteousness as a *gift*, it will outwardly manifest in our daily lives naturally and effortlessly. You will hear these truths repeated throughout the book because redundancy is a form of meditation - a key to living in victory over sin and temptation.

CHAPTER 5

Your Sin is Not "Covered" by the Blood

"WHAT? – How could you say the blood of Jesus doesn't cover our sin?!" I understand that most of us have been taught that the shed blood of Yeshua or Christ "covers" our sin, as though Yahweh were looking at us through "rose-colored glasses." Unfortunately, some have even taken this as an *excuse, justification,* or *license* for sin (e.g., "God knows I'm not perfect and that I'll always sin on some level until I die – besides, I'm 'covered' by the blood!"). However, you may have heard the funny but sad truth that most professing believers don't "need" a license to sin because they get along just fine *without* one. But listen, Yeshua's blood does <u>not</u> "cover" or "hide" our sin. We do see one verse in the New Testament that speaks of our sins being "covered," and that is Romans 4:7: *Blessed are those whose lawless deeds have been forgiven, and whose sins have been <u>covered</u>.* This is where it is important that we consider the context as well as the whole counsel of Scripture on this topic. For one, Paul is quoting Psalms 32:1, which was written *before* Yeshua's blood was shed and *before* the new covenant was established. The sins of believers who lived before Yeshua's sacrifice were merely *covered, hidden,* or *concealed* by the blood of animals, which could never remove or expiate sin or make them righteous and clean; it only provided *temporary* atonement, as the priests performed annual sacrifices on behalf of the people (See Heb.10:1-4). Secondly, the context of Romans 4 shows us that Paul was quoting Psalms 32 not to point out what happens to our sin, but to make the case that we are made righteous before God by *faith* and not by our obedience. He then explains in the proceeding chapters how the faith which cleanses us will

naturally *produce* the fruit of obedience or a practical and visible righteousness. The Scriptures clearly tell us that Yeshua is the "propitiation" of our sins, which does not mean to "cover" or "hide," but fully *satisfy, appease, relieve,* or *assuage.* It says the sacrifice of Yeshua "blotted out," "put away," or *removed* our sin, and that we "have been sanctified" (made holy) through the offering of Yeshua *once for all.*

We must understand that our Lord did not merely "bruise" or "bludgeon" the sin nature; He <u>eradicated</u> and <u>killed</u> it! (See Rom.3:25, 6:6-11; Heb. 2:17,9:26,10:10; 1 John 2:2; Acts 3:19 Rom.3:25, 6:6-11; Heb. 2:17,9:26,10:10; 1 John 2:2; Acts 3:19). You see, the animal sacrifices under the first covenant were not only insufficient to remove sin, but actually served to REMIND God's people of their sin year after year (Heb.10:3)! But when our Lord sacrificed Himself, it dealt with the sin problem and cleansed our consciences *once and for all!* As a result, not only was the annual reminder of sin and guilt through the shed blood of animals done away with– the blood of YESHUA perpetually reminds us of our forgiveness, cleansing, righteousness, wholeness, and healing! If we believe Yeshua merely "covers" our sin, as He did under the old covenant, we will either tolerate sin and just accept it, or try to kill or crucify it ourselves! Also, as noted earlier, we will also fall into either guilt/condemnation as we see our helplessness to overcome sin in our own strength, or we fall into pride/self-righteousness if we believe we're doing a "pretty good job" with managing sin and keeping His laws. We will later address the question that if the Lord truly killed our sin nature, how and why could we still sin? But for now, understand that sins which were "covered" by the blood of animals under the old covenant meant that only the person was *physically* and *temporarily* washed or cleansed; it was a *superficial, provisional,* and *short-term* cleansing. But sins which are "forgiven, blotted out, and put away" means our spirit, our body, AND conscience have been permanently spiritually cleansed and freed– which leads us to naturally live a pure and holy life (See Heb.9:13-14,10:22; 1 John 3:5,21). A cleansed conscience means the stain of our guilt, shame, and condemnation was fully removed – as well as the annual *reminder* of our sins through the sacrificial system! His blood and grace *empower* us to effortlessly live obedient and holy lives as we spiritually *rest* or "sink into" in the finished work of Yeshua! This rest is anything but passive or lazy; it is an *active* rest - one that inspires and empowers us to fulfill God's Word and will, as Paul said, *His grace toward me was not in vain, but I labored more abundantly than they all, yet <u>not I</u>, but the <u>grace of God which was with me</u>* (1 Cor.15:10). We could never *merit* a right standing with God or be justified by obedience, but just because we are righteous before God by *faith* does <u>not</u> negate His command for us to practically *flesh out* that righteousness (2 Cor.5:21; Rom.3:20). As we read in Matthew 3:8, *Therefore, produce <u>fruit</u> consistent with <u>repentance</u>,* keeping in mind that repentance has to do with changing our beliefs or how we think and "see," which in turn changes how we live.

Ultimately, it is God's *declaration* that we are righteous which physically and practically *brings us* into it, as Romans 4:17 says He speaks what <u>isn't</u> *as though it is*, which produces the manifestation! Of course, it will never manifest in our life if we are ignorant of the truth or if we fail to exercise our faith and cooperate with the Spirit of God. But understand this: while we can *outwardly* live a righteous life and not be inwardly righteous by *faith* in Yeshua, we <u>cannot</u> be righteous by faith *without* this outward and practical righteousness! Remember, while Paul said *no one* will be justified before God by keeping His Law, he also said that those who keep the Law are justified (Rom.3:20,2:13). In other words, you can't be made right with God by keeping His laws, but if you have been made right with Him by faith, you will keep His laws. Romans 1:5 and 16:25 talks about the *"obedience of faith,"* which means the true faith that makes us perfectly righteous before God will naturally yield *obedience* and a visible or tangible righteousness - not passivity or spiritual laziness and indifference. 2 Peter 3:14 and Philippians 2:12-13 say:

<u>*Make every effort*</u> *to be found spotless, blameless and at peace with Him;*

Work <u>out</u> your salvation with fear and trembling, for it is God who works <u>in</u> you, both to <u>will</u> and <u>act</u> for His good pleasure.

Such verses sound like salvation by works, but it's not about *earning* or working *for* our salvation or sanctification, but <u>cooperating</u> with and <u>yielding</u> to the Spirit's work in us, which obviously involves our choices and behavior. We are not puppets, and our spiritual growth does not happen automatically. Yahweh does not do everything for us because He wants to raise us up as His mature <u>sons</u>; because He gave us free will, we have the *responsibility* (and *privilege*) to pursue the Lord, His ways, and heart. But don't understand "responsibility" in the sense that <u>you</u> have to make it happen; to "do the works of God," your primary role is to *believe* or to have faith in the Lord - and even your faith is a gift (John 6:29; Eph.2:8-9)! When you rest in the Lord's finished work, His Spirit produces the fruit in and through you *without* striving. As Yeshua also said, when we abide or live in Him, we will bear *much* fruit!

What exactly is God's "good pleasure" that Paul mentions in the above verse? If we said "obedience," that is certainly true, but there is something that pleases Him more than outward conformity to His commands. What is that you may ask? Well, do you think God is pleased with our obedience when our motives or intentions are impure? As the Lord said in 1 Samuel 16:7 and Isaiah 29:13: *God does not see as man sees, since man looks at the outward appearance, but the Lord looks at the <u>heart</u>; "These people......honor Me with their lips, but their hearts are far from Me."* Many believers are motivated to obey God out of a sense of moral obligation or a legalistic and religious duty; others obey Him in hopeless attempts of *earning* His love or *meriting* His approval or even their salvation; still, as mentioned earlier, others obey Him because they are afraid and relate with God *not* as their Father, but more like a "Godfather" who is harsh, demanding, and always displeased with them. If earthly parents wouldn't be pleased or happy with their own children obeying them for such reasons, how much more would it be with our heavenly Father? What kind of parent says they don't care if their children obey them for the wrong reasons or that compliance is all that matters?

Obedience that is rooted in any other motive besides LOVE is what the Bible calls "dead works," because our works didn't spring from the key ingredient by which our faith works (Gal.5:6b). As Yeshua said in John 14:21, *"He who has My commandments and keeps them, he it is who <u>loves</u> Me."* The Pharisees of Yeshua's day proved it is possible for us to obey God's commands without truly loving or knowing Him, but it is <u>not</u> possible for us to truly love Him without obeying Him – as Yeshua goes on to say in verse 23, *"If anyone loves Me, he <u>will</u> keep My Word* (see also John 14:15). We know Hebrews 11:1 says *It is <u>impossible</u> to please God without <u>faith</u>.* But faith is not mere lip service or intellectual assent; faith causes the *positional* righteousness we have by grace and produces the fruit of practical obedience and holiness! And what is it that fuels or puts feet to faith? As we saw a moment ago, Paul put it this way in Galatians 5:6b and 2 Corinthians 5:14: *faith <u>works</u> through* LOVE; *the love of Christ compels us* [constrains, motivates, or inspires us]. And as we saw earlier in 1 John 5, because God's love transforms us, our obedience to Him is <u>not</u> burdensome, but rather a JOY, which makes it *effortless!* If we <u>desire</u> to do something, must we be *commanded* or *reminded* to do it? If we find it a pleasure to do something and we are motivated or inspired by love or passion to do it, it will *never* feel hard or heavy (1 John 5:3)! If it does, we do not have a true passion for it. If we really know Yahweh's love for us and we sincerely love Him, we need <u>no</u> reminders to be a "good Christian" or to live godly because love makes it *natural* and even *easy* for us to do so. The main point of this short chapter is this: the old you, along with your sins and sin nature, were not covered or concealed, but totally crucified and removed through your union with Christ. The more you mature in your revelation of this truth, the more your struggle with sin and temptation will become a thing of the past – and the more naturally and effortlessly it becomes for you to walk in obedience, holiness, and righteousness!

CHAPTER 6

Aren't we Living in the "Age of Grace"?

We're going to talk about grace in this chapter because if we fail to rightly understand its role and intended effect in our lives, as Paul said, we can receive it in vain (2 Cor.6:1). Many Christians believe Yahweh didn't truly reveal or show His grace until Yeshua came, quoting John 1:17 - *For the law was given through Moses, grace and truth came through Jesus.* They interpret this to mean that before Yeshua stepped onto the scene, believers lived during the age of "law/ works," and after He came, believers were ushered into the age of "grace/faith." Some translations even insert the word "but" in the middle of the verse, as if there was a tension between Yahweh's laws and grace and truth, but such reasoning is clearly erroneous because God said His Law is not only *true,* but <u>truth</u> itself (Neh.9:13; Ps.19:9; Rom.2:20). However, let us look at the context by considering the verse right before it. Verse 16 says, *"And from His fullness, we have all received grace upon grace."* The NIV renders it: *"Out of His fullness we have all received grace in place of grace already given."* What grace was "already given"? The next verse tells us: the Law of God given through Moses. Most Christians would say, *"What? God's Law is the <u>opposite</u> of His grace!"* This assertion is often based on verses like Galatians 5:4, where Paul says if we seek to be justified by law, we have "fallen from grace."

If we are trying to earn our salvation or justification through law-keeping, then we have indeed "fallen from grace" because we are guilty of trusting in ourselves, but it is a grave error to believe God's laws and His grace somehow oppose one another! They *can* "oppose" one another, but only when we try to earn His grace or favor *through* keeping His Law (see Rom.11:6; Gal.2:21). But we know it was an act of grace for Yahweh to give His Law, not only because it reveals our spiritually lost and dead state, but because it is a source of wisdom and guidance for us, which in turn helps preserve, protect, and bless our lives when observing it in the context of a love relationship with Him. And most of all, as His Law reveals our sin, it also points us to our only Source of salvation, Yeshua, preparing or conditioning our hearts to receive Him! (See Rom.3:20; Jer.31:2; Deut.5:33, 6:24, 15:5-6, 29:9, 30:8-9; Ex.34:6; Num.6:25).

Knowing this, John cannot be suggesting that before Yeshua came, Yahweh was not a God of grace or that His laws were in tension with truth and grace. If John was implying that Yahweh changed His nature or mood after Calvary, that would mean Yahweh *does* change and *does* alter His words, even though He clearly says He does <u>not</u> (Mal.3:6; Ps.89:34; Num.23:19). We read in the Old Testament many times where Yahweh declares His Law to be truth, and we see many instances where He shows grace, compassion, mercy, and favor to His people in spite of their sin, rebellion, and unbelief. Nehemiah chapter 9 is a perfect example of this. Since Yahweh said He never changes and that His Law is true, grace will forever be a core facet of His nature. Yeshua prayed in John 17:17, *"Sanctify them by the truth."* What "truth"? The second half of the verse says, *"Your <u>Word</u> is truth."* Ephesians 5:26 affirms this, telling us that we are "washed" or "cleansed" by the Word. Because Yeshua is the embodiment and exact representation of Yahweh's being, Word and Truth, John 1:17 cannot be interpreted to mean that He came to oppose the Law or *replace* it with grace and truth – especially when we understand that Yahweh's Law <u>is</u> truth and that giving His laws to us was an amazing act of grace and love!

Do we really believe the Messiah would spend His entire ministry teaching and exhorting from the Law of Moses (and correcting misinterpretations and abuses of it), only to discard or negate it, making it bad, harmful, wrong, or foolish to practice? Do we really believe He kept the Law so His followers would be absolved from keeping it – particularly when we are commanded to walk in His footsteps or follow His example? Surely, Yeshua came to flawlessly keep the Law in order to atone for our sins by His sacrifice, but as Galatians 2:17 says, He is not a "minister of sin"! In other words, His blood and grace didn't cleanse us from sin and free us from the law of sin and death so we can continue living in sin, which the Bible defines as the transgression of His Law (1 John 3:4; Rom.6:1-2)! He kept the Law not only to provide atonement, but to show us how to walk with the Father and keep His commandments in the manner He always intended: *through a relationship with Him rooted in love and faith, empowered by His Spirit and grace* - not out of a sense of duty, and not *for* salvation but as the *fruit* of our salvation (Deut.11:1/Is.29:13/ Zech.4:6). Yeshua modeled for us how to live out the Law *in the spirit of truth and grace motivated by love* – not in a spirit of legalism, licentiousness, hypocrisy, passivity or rigidity, and self-righteousness. He revealed the true intent of the Law – how it was never meant to be used as a "self-help manual" or to exploit, control and manipulate others as the Pharisees did (and many still do today).

If believers were in the "age of Law" before Yeshua, why did Yahweh make it clear in Ezekiel 33 and Deuteronomy 9 that it was not *their* righteousness which saved or delivered them, but because of HIS faithfulness to the covenant He made with them? Why does Hebrews 11 say the "ancients" or "men of old" gained God's approval through *faith*, <u>not</u> the Law or their works? Remember, the Lord tells us that Abraham, who had the gospel preached to him and who was righteous by faith, longed to see His day and saw it with joy, and the Law does not oppose God's promises or His grace and faithfulness (Gal.3:8,21; Rom.4:13; John 8:56). The truth is, our salvation, redemption or justification was <u>never</u> rooted in our obedience – neither *before* nor *after* Yeshua came. Grace is not a new facet of God's nature that wasn't revealed until Calvary. It has always been about faith and Yahweh's grace, as Paul said in Romans 3:21-24:

But now <u>apart from the Law</u> the righteousness of God has been manifested, being witnessed by the <u>Law and the Prophets,</u> even the righteousness of God <u>through faith</u> in Jesus Christ for all those who believe.....being justified as a <u>gift</u> by His <u>grace</u> through the redemption which is in Christ Jesus.

But this does not mean there is no correlation between grace/faith and works/obedience, or that we must choose between the two. The Bible explicitly teaches that while it is possible for us to *religiously* keep God's laws without saving faith and living "under grace," it is NOT possible for us to have biblical faith and be living "under grace" *without* naturally living a life of godliness and *joyful* obedience. Grace and faith, which are the only <u>root</u> of our salvation, will never fail to produce the *fruit* of obedience and holiness. Grace does not give us a license to sin, rather, grace frees us *from* sin or delivers us from its dominion, empowering us to live holy, obedient lives (out of desire and delight, not out of duty and drudgery)! And as Paul said in Romans 3:31, faith does <u>not</u> nullify the Law or make it obsolete, but it *establishes* it, making us an embodiment of the Word. These are fundamental truths and characteristics of a biblical or saving faith. If it were true that believers who live after Christ's sacrifice are under grace in the sense that their lives don't need to reflect the righteousness of God expressed in His Word or laws, and if Christ's teachings truly show us that His Father's nature, temperament, and expectations *changed*, why do we see examples all throughout the NEW Testament of God's judgment, anger, and wrath? For instance:

> Yeshua said a servant who knew his master's will but disobeyed will be "severely beaten" and those who did not know will still be beaten, yet less severely (Luke 12). This doesn't mean the Lord "beats" us, but He surely *disciplines* His children. Those misled by the doctrine of "cheap-grace" expect <u>zero</u> consequence for their sin and disobedience because of Calvary. Yeshua also said the cities He visited that did not repent will be worse off than Sodom and Gomorrah! [Matt.11] We may have escaped *judgement* for our sin because Yeshua stood in our place for that, but that doesn't mean we aren't *disciplined.*

> Two believers (not lost sinners) died on the spot for their greed and deception [Acts 5].

> God's wrath is "stored up" for the godless or "sons of disobedience" and there will be "judgment, tribulation and distress" for those who practice evil and do "not obey the truth." [Rom.1 & 2; Col.3:6]

> Peter condemned a man to *destruction* for trying to "buy" God's power to heal the sick [Acts 8]. Paul also delivered a man over to Satan for the *destruction* of his flesh or body because of sexual sin [1 Cor.5].

> Yeshua says His return will be like the time Yahweh brought judgment on the earth through the flood and raining down fire and brimstone on Sodom and Gomorrah [Luke 17].

> Upon His return, Yeshua will be revealed from heaven with "flaming fire, dealing out retribution" to the *disobedient*, who will "pay the penalty of eternal destruction" [2 Thess.1].

> God judged and disciplined many believers with sickness or even death for taking Communion unworthily (failing to examine and judge themselves through repentance) [1 Cor.11:28-30].

> We can expect "judgment" and a "fury of fire" to "consume" those who willfully continue sinning after receiving the knowledge of the truth [Heb.10:26].

> Acts 12:23 says that because king Herod did not give glory to God, an angel of the Lord "struck" him with a deadly disease.

> Hebrews 10:28-31 says: *Anyone who has set aside the law of Moses dies without mercy on the evidence of two or three witnesses. How much worse punishment, do you think, will be deserved by the one who has trampled underfoot the Son of God, and has profaned the blood of the covenant by which he was sanctified, and has outraged the Spirit of grace? For we know him who said, "Vengeance is mine; I will repay." And again, "The Lord will judge his people." It is a fearful thing to fall into the hands of the living God!* We are not to live in "tormenting fear" of God's judgment, as His love casts out such fear, but we are to have a *pure* and *holy* fear or reverence of Him and His Word.

> Revelation 16 speaks of God's "bowls of wrath" in the End Days, when He destroys entire cities with disease, earthquakes, fire and huge hailstones for rebellion and disobedience.

> 1 Peter 4:17-18 says *judgment begins with the household of God, and if it begins with us first, what will be the outcome for those who do not obey the gospel of God? If it is with difficulty that the righteous is saved, what will become of the godless man and sinner?* Some Christians equate the liberty we have in Christ with escaping God's judgment of our sin because we are "covered by grace," but verses like 1 Peter 2:16 and Galatians 5:13 equate our liberty with <u>obedience</u> to God and holiness. Yes, we escape God's *wrath* if we are in Yeshua, but both of Peter's letters are filled with examples of how God's people are to live holy and obedient lives, and that judgment and wrath will come upon not only *lost sinners*, but also those who profess to know God but who's lives fail to reflect and affirm it. This is why we are to "make our calling and election sure," "testing" or "examining" ourselves to see if we are truly in the faith (2 Pet.1:5-11; 2 Cor.13:5).

> If we are unforgiving or bitter towards those who sin against us, our sins will not be forgiven and God will hand us over to "tormentors" (demons) which harass/afflict us (Matt.6:15,18:33-34).

> Yeshua told a man He healed in John 5 to *stop* sinning so that nothing *worse* would happen to him. Does such a statement support the "Age of grace" or that the idea that sin no longer leads to bad consequences in our lives? Yes, this man was still living "under" the Old Covenant

because the New Covenant had not yet been established or instituted through Yeshua's sacrifice, but what the Lord told this man is based on the *everlasting* principle of sowing and reaping (Gal.6:7; Jer.40:3,44:5-6,23).

Most of these passages of Scripture were written <u>after</u> Yeshua's sacrifice and ascension, and none of these instances sound different from how God dealt with sin and rebellion before Yeshua established the new covenant. The truth is, Yahweh will never change what He thinks about sin and how He deals with it; He has always been "slow to anger and abounding in lovingkindness," never "taking pleasure in the death of the wicked" or "willing that any should perish," but He disciplines and/or judges when needed. Thankfully, His grace always pardons those who repent and turn back to Him and His ways, as the Old Testament gives many examples of His grace, mercy, and compassion. But just like the New Testament, which affirms and stands upon the "Old," it also shows that He is righteous, holy, just, and changeless. As Yeshua said, until heaven and earth pass away, His command for us to walk in holiness and obedience to His laws will stand, and not only will rebellious unbelievers be judged, but also those who profess to know Him yet who practice sin in their lives or have a casual attitude towards it. But what about Paul's words in 2 Corinthians 5:19 and Romans 5:18-19, which say:

....God was in Christ, reconciling the world to Himself, <u>not counting their trespasses against them</u>, and He has committed to us the word [ministry] of reconciliation.

For if, because of one man's trespass, death reigned through that one man (Adam), much more will those who receive the <u>abundance of grace and the free gift of righteousness</u> reign in life through the one man Jesus Christ. Therefore, as one trespass led to condemnation for all men, so <u>one act of righteousness leads to justification and life for all men</u>.

These verses are often used to support the belief that the "Age of Law" has passed, and that Yeshua's sacrifice ushered us into the "Age of Grace" (as Dispensationalism teaches). Taken at face value and out of context, they are also used to support the teachings of Universalism – the belief that all of humanity throughout all of history are automatically saved and go to heaven when they die. But when we consider the whole counsel of Scripture and allow the Word to interpret itself, we find such teaching to be blatantly unscriptural. These are the questions we need to ask: is Paul saying God's view and treatment of our sin (violation of His Law) changed after Calvary, or that because believers are reconciled with their heavenly Father, He no longer punishes or disciplines them for violating His Word or Law? Is he saying the "world" or all of humanity not only potentially, but literally, has been "justified" and "reconciled" to God – meaning they are in right standing with Him and that they no longer stand under God's judgment and condemnation for their sin?

If Paul was saying any of these things, he would be contradicting himself and indeed promoting Universalism. If an unbeliever's sins are not counted against them *automatically*, that obviously means God has made that person right with Him (past tense), which in turn means they are *already* saved and have *already* been rescued from judgment. If reconciliation with Yahweh was automatic because of Yeshua's sacrifice, it would make no sense for Paul to say in the same verse that God has *"committed to us the word (or ministry) of reconciliation,"* and in the next verse: *"we implore (or beg) you on behalf of Christ, be reconciled to God"* (2 Cor.5:19-20). If we have been automatically reconciled to our heavenly Father because of what Yeshua did, the "ministry of reconciliation" would clearly serve no purpose, and we would not need to share the gospel or "implore" people to "be reconciled" with God.

Paul surely wrote under the inspiration of God's Spirit, so he is right – the Lord indeed "reconciled the world to Himself" through Yeshua's sacrifice. But his writings, along with the entire Word of God, make it clear that each of us is must personally respond to and *receive* this free gift of grace made available to us (e.g., Rom.5:17). The glorious benefits of Yeshua's sacrifice do not come to us automatically; in His death, a legal transaction and verdict was rendered – the verdict being: reconciliation with our heavenly Father (and freedom from sin and its dominion over us) has been made possible and available to all. How? Because He has "taken away the sins of the world" and "no longer counts our sins against us" (John 1:29; 1 John 2:2; 2 Cor.5:19). However, if unbelievers don't know this truth or reject it, they will still be judged. Why? Because when a judge renders a verdict or judgment in a court of law, they do not step down from their bench to enforce it; that is not their responsibility, as there are others who must take the legal rendering of the judge and enforce or execute it so that it has practical ramifications. Until the judge's verdict is applied or appropriated and enforced, it has NO functional or practical power – even though it has legally been rendered. Likewise, just because God has forgiven us of our sin does not mean we can trivialize His laws or go back to living according to the patterns of the "old man" (why would we want to do that if we now share in God's nature?). Nor does it mean there are no natural consequences for sin, as 1 Peter 4:17 says: *judgment begins with the household of God, and if it starts with us. What will be the fate of those who refuse to obey the gospel of God?* Hebrews 4:13 and 9:27 also say that *no creature is hidden from His sight, but all are naked and exposed to the eyes of Him to whom we must give account,* and *that all men will face judgment after death.*

1 Thessalonians 5:9 says we are "not appointed for wrath" because Yeshua received the ultimate judgment we deserved, but that does not mean Yahweh no longer disciplines us for our sin or holds us accountable, as 2 Corinthians 5:10 and Romans 14:10 say we must all appear before the judgment seat of God or Christ (known as the Great White Throne Judgment). As our Father, Yahweh indeed holds us *accountable,* indeed *disciplines* us, and indeed *will judge* us. Why? Scripture says it is so that we will not be condemned along with the world, that we may share in His holiness, and that we may have *confidence* in the day of judgment (1 Cor.11:32; Heb.12:10; 1 Jhn.4:17). And He surely holds the unbelieving world accountable for sin, rebellion, and unbelief, as Paul says He is "storing up wrath" and will judge those who do not repent and do "not obey the truth." But it is important to understand that Yahweh's judgment of His *people* has nothing to do with their <u>sin</u>, which was dealt with through Yeshua's sacrifice, but with the *rewards* He gives them at the end of the age for their faithful service and the things they accomplished for His glory and kingdom (Matt.16:27; Rev.22:12; 1 Cor.3:8). He surely *disciplines* us for sin, but does not *judge* or *condemn* us for it. As noted, 2 Corinthians 5:19 indeed says Yahweh is "not counting" man's sins against them, but we cannot interpret that in a way which contradicts other scriptures, such as the fact that when Yeshua returns, He is returning to JUDGE the <u>world</u> for its *sin*, and that His Father's wrath will be poured out in terrible and utterly devastating ways, as described in the book of Revelation. The God we see in what we call the "Old Testament" is no different than the God we see in Revelation and who we worship and serve today; Why do you think He is called the "God of Abraham, Isaac and Jacob"? It is to convey the truth that His nature is immutable, that He is faithful to all His Name stands for, and that He will never alter His Word, standards, and expectations! (See Mal.3:6; Heb.13:8; Ps.89:34)

At this point, hopefully you can see the dangers of "easy-believism" – the idea that *"All you must do to be saved is believe in Jesus and call on His Name or confess Him as Lord."* Again, that is a true statement from Scripture (Rom.10:9,13), but we cannot divorce it from the rest of what the Bible says concerning the nature of faith and salvation. As we have noted several times, we *must* read Scripture in context and allow the Word of God to interpret itself, and if your faith in Yeshua does not increasingly produce the God-glorifying fruit of obedience and sanctification, your faith is dead (see 2 Peter 1:8)! As the letter of 1 John explicitly tells us, if our confession of Him as Lord and Savior does not outwardly manifest the nature and character of God expressed in His Word, our confession is mere lip service, and we make ourselves out to be a liar![12]

Why do so many Christians live in a perpetual struggle to overcome sin and temptation, and why does it seem next to impossible for them to live holy, set-apart lives? While it is possible it is because they are not truly born-again or spiritually regenerated, it is more likely due to false and self-destructive doctrines they have learned. I know this firsthand, because I spent many years of my walk with the Lord in a never-ending battle with habitual sin. I felt trapped, helpless, and hopeless – and I eventually came to the point where I wondered what's the point of even trying anymore? I wasn't caught up in what most would consider "gross" sins of immorality or the "nasty nine and dirty dozen" type of sins, but that didn't matter because Yahweh hates ALL sin. But I still felt like a condemned "dirty-rotten sinner" who had no choice but to tolerate habitual sin in my life. I speak for myself, but I believe the reason I constantly fought to overcome besetting sin is the same reason most Christians fight or struggle to overcome sin and temptation. Again, I do not believe the main reason believers struggle with sin is because they are <u>not</u> truly born-again, and certainly <u>not</u> because they don't sincerely love God and desire to honor Him; it is primarily due to *false teaching* and *wrong thoughts, beliefs, and confessions*. As noted in the preface of this book, **all sin is ultimately a problem with _belief_ and _identity_, not behavior.** For instance, if you have been in the traditional church setting for any length of time, you were likely led to believe that even for followers of Christ, sinning is *normal* and even *expected*. Why? Because as previously noted, we are told that we are "only human," and if saints like Paul apparently struggled with it, then you can bet *we* will too! Besides, didn't God give His Law and the 10 Commandments to show His people how *sinful* they are and that they are *helpless* to observe them?

This is a packed question on a huge topic that can take us in many directions, but we will touch on it again here: under the inspiration of Holy Spirit, Paul tells us in Romans 3:20 that indeed, one of the purposes of the Law, as we have already seen, is to make humanity aware of their sinful or morally and spiritually depraved state. He also said the Law reveals how heinous sin truly is, as well as how God's grace reigns and abounds over sin (Ch.5,v.20). He then explains in chapter 6 how God's grace does not give us an excuse for continuing to sin, but that it *delivers* or *frees* us from sin's dominion and transforms and empowers us to live righteously (keeping in mind that God's Law is precisely what *defines* righteousness). But it is vital to understand that when God gave His Law, it was made clear in Deuteronomy 30:11 that the commandments were NOT "too difficult" to keep, as 1 John 5:3 affirms when it says God's commandments are not "burdensome." If this is true, why did Israel keep violating Yahweh's laws or have such difficulty observing them? God's people kept breaking His laws not because they were unreasonable or "impossible to keep" as most believers erroneously claim; neither was it because they had a lot of religious baggage and false doctrines floating around like we do today. Rather, it was because their *hearts* or *spirits* were not in the right place. For example, the Lord said of Caleb, *"He has a _different_* _spirit_ in him and has followed Me _fully_"; the Scriptures speak of Noah as a _righteous_ man, _blameless_ in his generation, and Job as a man who was _blameless_ and _upright,_ who feared God and turned from evil; The Lord also said of Abraham and John the Baptist's parents, _"Abraham obeyed My voice and kept My charge, My commandments, statutes and laws"; "they were both _righteous_ in the sight of God, walking _blamelessly_ in all the commandments and requirements of the Lord_ (Num.14:23; Gen.6:9,26:5; Job 1:1; Luke 1:6).

Notice how most of these are examples are from the Old Testament, _before_ Yeshua renewed the covenant and sent His Spirit to permanently indwell and empower His people! But new covenant believers, who "can do ALL things through Christ" and for whom "all things are possible," have the audacity to say, _"We _cannot_ keep the Law – it's too difficult and heavy!"_ If our hearts have been transformed and we have become born-again new creations in Yeshua who are filled with His _Holy_ Spirit, how can we possibly say things like this? Has our heart not been _circumcised_ and _transformed_ to _delight_ in Yahweh's laws[13], and does the Lord not work in us to _desire_ and _act_ according to His good pleasure – which of course is living in obedience to His commands? (See Ezek.11:19-20; Phil.2:13; 1 John 3:22). If we're talking about keeping God's Law to earn _salvation,_ then of course, that's impossible because we would have to do it perfectly as Yeshua did. But when most believers say they "can't keep" God's laws, they're using that as an excuse for routine or habitual sin in their lives.

The reason so many Christians struggle with sin is clearly because they do not know the Word of God, or if they do, it is confined to mere head knowledge or ink on paper. This proves my point that wrong beliefs produce wrong living and that our behavior (the fruit) cannot rise above the level of our beliefs and confessions (the root)! No matter how hard we try, if our inner conviction is that we are "sinners" and that God's Law is "impossible to keep," just as water always finds its level, our outward lives and habits will eventually fall back to align or agree with those core beliefs. If our conviction is that we "can't keep God's Law" and that its sole purpose is to perpetually remind us of our depravity or keep us in a sin-conscious state, we shouldn't be surprised of the rotten fruit that such thinking and confessions will produce. As Proverbs 18:20 says:

With the fruit of a man's mouth will his stomach be satisfied; he is satisfied with the product of his lips.

Yeshua affirms this in Luke 6:45:

A <u>good</u> man, out of the <u>good treasure</u> of his heart brings forth <u>good</u>; and an <u>evil</u> man, out of the <u>evil treasure</u> of his heart brings forth <u>evil</u>. <u>For out of the abundance of the heart, his mouth speaks</u>.

This is why Proverbs 4:23 tells us to: *Guard our heart, for ALL we do flows from it!* Perhaps you were falsely taught, as I was, that when the Bible says your old carnal sinful nature was "crucified with Christ" and that you have been made a "new creation" in Him, you were to understand that in *spiritual* or *doctrinal* terms only, rather than in a literal and practical sense - at least not until you physically died and went to heaven. I don't know about you, but I was told I should accept as <u>fact</u> that the sinful nature we inherited from Adam wasn't *truly* dead and that my union with Christ and His death wasn't going to have a practical application as long as I was in this "meat sack" called a body. I eventually concluded that while my desires and efforts to live a life free from sin were godly and noble, they were simply ill-founded and based on a misunderstanding and misapplication of Scripture. I had become so far removed from the truth of Scripture on this topic that I had come to believe that if anyone said it's not only *possible* for us to live a life free from sin, but that it's God's perfect <u>will</u> and <u>desire</u> that we do so, they were deceived, self-righteous heretics who either forgot (or just didn't know) how sinful, sick, wicked and depraved their hearts truly were!![14]

It's no wonder that I struggled to overcome sin with such a mentality! What I had become thoroughly convinced of through false doctrine shaped my core beliefs to the point that I reluctantly, unintentionally, and subconsciously began to *tolerate* sin in my life, which in turn began to *dominate* and *control* me! While the Word tells me to be *renewed* in the spirit of my mind, I was unwittingly doing the opposite through wrong and deceptive thoughts – which led me to act in alignment with my mind. My body had "become" my mind, so to speak, and I found myself subconsciously stuck in an "auto-pilot" cycle of wrong thoughts, feelings, and actions, which in turn produced more wrong thoughts, feelings, and actions! This isn't based on some weird and heretical teaching, but is based on Scripture and spiritual/physical axioms that *God* established. For instance, Jeremiah 6:19 speaks of "calamity" coming upon us by "the fruit of our thoughts," and as I will often repeat, we *perish* or go into *exile* for our lack of knowledge (Hosea 4:6; Is.5:13). In chapter eight, we will take a more detailed look into how our beliefs, words, and actions inseparably work together to create our state of being and reality, but before we do so, it is imperative that we understand the role of God's Law in our lives and how He intends for us to relate with it.

CHAPTER 7

God's Law and You

We touched on this earlier, but we need to dig a little deeper on this subject – and this chapter is quite lengthy because it is vital that we understand it. Due to false teaching, many Christians have a unhealthy and even damaging "relationship" with God's Law by either using it "illegally" or believing it was made obsolete through Christ because He "fulfilled" it.[15] But as noted previously, how can we live a "godly" or "righteous" life and walk in "obedience" if God's laws, which define righteousness, have been done away with? As much as the Church respects Paul, who wrote two thirds of the New Testament, we must remember that he said God's Law <u>itself</u> is *good, righteous,* and even *spiritual* – that is, when we relate with it *legally* or as God intended, and that faith doesn't nullify the Law, but *establishes* it (Rom.7:12-14, 3:31; 1 Tim.1:8). And if we know our Bibles, we understand that Yeshua Himself <u>is</u> the *embodiment* of the Word of God, as He perfectly "fleshed out," modeled, and taught the righteousness of Yahweh's commands (John 1:1,14; Matt.5:17-20). This means we cannot claim to follow the Lord and live as though Yeshua, the Living Word, is separate from the Law of God, the written Word. The truth that our Lord is the personification and manifestation of the Word of God should make it obvious that the two are inseparable. However, the Scriptures clearly teach that while it is possible that we can mentally know the Word well and endeavor to be "good law-keepers" without truly knowing the Lord (see John 5:39), it is <u>not</u> possible to have a true love relationship with Him *without* keeping His laws and rightly relating with His Word or Law – where we *delight* in His ways and *desire* to reflect His nature in all we do.

So, whether we realize it or not, *all* of us have a "relationship" with God's Law or Word, and understanding the nature of that relationship will tell us whether our relationship with the <u>God</u> of that Law is on solid or shaky ground. Many believers are convinced that the foundation of their relationship with God is solid, but if you were to ask some questions concerning their motives for *why* they seek to obey His Word and live righteous lives, and *why* they are confident they are "heaven-bound," you might hear answers that do not align with Scripture or with the nature of faith and salvation. And worse, many believe they are "rotten sinners who sin all the time," and while they agree that walking in God's Word or commands is surely good and right, it isn't necessary or really important because they are saved by grace and not by works. "Besides," they say, "because we are such weak sinners, we can't keep the Law anyway," which implies, "why even try"? So, the question is: do you relate with the Law of God in a healthy or <u>un</u>healthy way - a biblical way or <u>un</u>biblical way? Do you seek to obey it in a way that God intended, or in a way He did <u>not</u> intend, which will harm, condemn, and ultimately bring spiritual death? Or do you believe that because of what Jesus did for you, it isn't that important that your life reflects the righteousness of God's Word and that you seek to walk in victory over sin and temptation – a victory that's already been given to you? Or lastly, do you believe it *is* important, but you feel powerless to keep it because you see yourself as weak or identify yourself as a captive enslaved to sin? These are vital questions to ask, and more importantly, to have biblically *answered,* as this chapter aims to do.

As I've alluded to, many do not understand that we can relate with God's Law in a wrong or harmful way and use it in a manner He did <u>not</u> intend. Without being aware of it, those who are prone to self-righteousness and pride use God's Law to boost their ego and give them a sense of spiritual and moral superiority (e.g., the

Pharisee who says, "I thank God I'm not like those 'sinners'!"). On the other hand, those who are prone to self-introspection see the Law as a wagging "finger in the face" that constantly condemns them by pointing out their flaws and reminding them of how far they fall from measuring up to God's standards (e.g., "I'm such a screw-up!"). We may not walk in a spirit of pride or condemnation, but it is possible that we are religiously trying to keep the Law because it is our "duty," believing that conformity to God's laws is what really matters in the end.

Something you will hear me say several times is that Yahweh is not impressed with mere behavior modification or outward conformity to His Word and He hates obedience that is fueled by the flesh, a sense of duty, or pride, unbelief, and self-righteousness. Such obedience is considered "dead works" in God's sight because those works were not a fruit of His Spirit but of our fleshly attempts to appease God. He never intended for us to relate with His Law in *any* of these ways, as they bring us under condemnation and judgment, ultimately leading to our death. "Unbelief" is included in the above list because if we are wallowing in guilt, shame, and condemnation for our sin or failures, it is because we do not *truly* believe the good news of the Gospel – that we are indeed *forgiven, cleansed, transformed,* and *empowered* to live holy by the blood of Yeshua and His indwelling Spirit! And keep this in mind: unbelief can also manifest itself through pride and self-righteousness. How? If your standing before God rests in *your* performance and not *Yeshua's,* you clearly do <u>not</u> believe or have faith in HIS righteousness!

From Which Tree Are You Eating?

We touched on this earlier, but when we are using and relating with the Law in any of the above manners, it is because we are partaking from the ***Tree of the Knowledge of Good and Evil,*** rather than the ***Tree of Life***. Surely you recall that Yahweh placed these two trees in the Garden of Eden (Gen.2:9). The Tree of Life represents Yeshua, as He said He is the Way, the Truth, and "the Life," and that He gives us a full and abundant life (John 14:7, 10:10). That abundant life represents salvation, forgiveness, intimacy with our Lord, righteousness, provision, the fruit of the Spirit, and prosperity and healing of our spirit, soul, and body (and all that God's kingdom entails). The Tree of the Knowledge of Good and Evil represents just that – the knowledge, awareness, or consciousness of good AND evil. Living with an awareness of good and evil seems perfectly normal for us because humanity has known nothing different since the Fall, but think about it: Before Adam and Eve chose to listen to Satan and eat from this tree, all they were aware or conscious of was goodness, righteousness, holiness, beauty, God's glory, love, peace, joy, etc., having *no* conception or comprehension of sin and evil, along with the awful effect it could have on them and the world. Of course, because Satan had already rebelled against Yahweh, sin and evil *did* exist, but Adam and Eve weren't aware of that because it wasn't yet manifested in the world. But when they ate of this tree, Scripture says their "eyes were opened" (spiritual eyes) and they knew they were "naked".[16]

When we "eat" or live from the Tree of the Knowledge of Good and Evil, or relate with God through His Law, we are trying to use the very thing that got us in trouble to get back what was lost. But if eating from that tree got us evicted from the Garden, how could "eating" from it get us back in? Behavior modification and outward conformity to the Law is not the answer or goal. If we live as though our good performance can qualify us before God, we come under the judgment and condemnation of the Law. But if we are partaking from the Tree of Life, Yeshua Himself, we understand that if our good performance can never qualify us, we know our poor performance can never *disqualify* us. Knowing this doesn't lead to loose living, but the opposite because our motivation is love and gratitude, not fear, duty, or legalism! You see, God's greatest desire is <u>not</u> that we simply conform to His laws. If that were the case, Yeshua would have been very pleased with the religious leaders of His day. Yahweh's greatest desire is that we intimately KNOW Him, and out of that intimacy, be conformed into His very image, becoming an embodiment of the Word and the exact representation of His nature![17]

You may ask, *"But doesn't God's Law reflect His nature, and doesn't God expect and command us to keep His laws?"* Of course, but remember, Yeshua said that unless our righteousness exceeds the righteousness of the scribes and Pharisees, we will not enter His kingdom (Matt.5:20). In other words, if our righteousness is only skin-deep and our focus is on law-keeping and outward conformity to God's standards, rather than inner transformation and intimacy with Him, we remain blind to the glory of Yahweh in His Son, as well as to our true identity in Him. As the Word says, when we do not know who we are in the Lord, a veil remains over the eyes of our hearts when the Old Covenant is read, but when we turn to Him, that veil is lifted so that we can see the glory of the Lord, and as we behold His glory, He transforms us into His image from glory to glory (2 Cor.3:14-18). You see, the Law cannot reveal our true identity in the Lord – it can only reveal our sin and tell us what to do (and what not to do), and how to avoid sin. It also provides physical protection and mitigates the damaging effects sin has on our bodies when we observe it, but it was never designed to give us *spiritual* life and transformation, nor place us in right standing with God.

You must understand that the Gospel doesn't reveal what <u>you</u> need to do to solve your problem with sin; it reveals what has *already been done* to solve your problem! If you are united to Yeshua by faith, sharing in His death and resurrection, you have *already arrived* at where you're straining to get to, and you *already have* what you are tirelessly striving to obtain. If you work to obtain that which has already been given to you by grace through faith, you unwittingly keep yourself from ever stepping into it because you are vainly attempting to earn or pay for a *gift*. **If you use it illegally or in a way God never intended, the Law of God will actually *hinder* or *deter* you from manifesting or living out who He says you <u>already</u> are by grace through faith.** Religious people hate that statement because they believe we can't be holy or live righteously without God's laws keeping us in check, but it is the height of arrogance to think we could merit a righteousness of our own by "climbing the ladder" of God's Law. "Do it yourself" religion is a harsh and demanding taskmaster that keeps you living "under the Law" by partaking of the wrong tree, where you become introspective and self-focused, always judging yourself to assess whether or not you're performing well enough to qualify for God's promises, blessings, unconditional love and acceptance – and then you have to tirelessly *maintain* that position! So, if you *do* know who you are in the Lord, do not make the mistake the believers in Galatia did by relying on your law-keeping in vain efforts to become who you *already* are or to obtain and *maintain* what has *already* been given you by grace through faith in the <u>perfect</u> and <u>finished</u> work of Yeshua!

It is also important to note that if you believe Yeshua died *because* of you rather than FOR you, you will believe you *owe* God and will therefore try to obtain by the flesh what has already been given to you as a gift (again, you can't pay for a gift, and you could never pay him back anyway)! If Yeshua said *no one* takes His life, but that He laid it down *willingly* or *of His own accord*, that means you didn't "kill" him or that you aren't to "blame" for His death (John 10:18). Also, if we believe we have to do something to become who we already are by our union with Yeshua, we will "hide" and make excuses for not cultivating deeper intimacy with Yahweh when He "shows up to walk with us" like He did with Adam in the Garden. When we speak of "not going back to law-keeping," we are <u>not</u> talking about abandoning the Law or living disobedient, ungodly, and sinful lives. That should be obvious, but the second half of the previous sentence is the key: we don't go back to law-keeping *in efforts to become who we <u>already are</u> or to obtain what we <u>already have</u> by GRACE through FAITH <u>alone</u>!* What is it that we already have, and who is it that we already are? We are born-again SONS of God and are *one* with Yeshua and new creations in Him who share His very nature – and because of this truth, our lives will automatically reflect the righteousness and glory of our Father expressed in His commands, where we don't even need to be told what to do or how to act because His Word has taken on flesh again in <u>us</u>![18] I hope this has helped you understand how vital is that you have a *right* relationship with God and His Law, and how vital it is <u>not</u> to use His Word or law "illegally".

The Bible says God's Law is NOT for Righteous People??

Paul makes an interesting statement in 1 Timothy 1:9, saying God's Law was "not made for a righteous man, but for *lawless, rebellious,* and *ungodly <u>sinners</u>.*" It should go without saying that Paul does <u>not</u> mean that if we are righteous by our faith in the Lord, we can live as law-breakers, for the obvious reason that we can't live "righteously" if we aren't observing the very laws that *define* and *reflect* righteousness. The righteousness and salvation we have is by grace through faith alone in the finished work of Yeshua, but our faith is never truly "alone" in the sense that it is always *accompanied* by the fruit of our obedience or good works, which is produced not by religious duty, but as we saw earlier, by *faith* through <u>love</u>.[19] He affirms this in verse 5, *the goal of our instruction is <u>love from a pure heart</u> and a good conscience and a <u>sincere</u> faith*. He did <u>not</u> say the goal of instruction is mere obedience or conformity to God's laws; he said the goal is LOVE, because when *love* for God is our goal, and we are enjoying and cultivating intimacy with Him, the seed of love will naturally yield the fruit of obedience. As Yeshua said, if we *love* Him, we will *keep* His commands.

Paul is saying a truly righteous person does not "need" a list of rules telling them what is right or wrong and good or evil; they don't "need" the Law of God to act like a school master, guardian, or tutor looming over them, constantly keeping them in check and reminding them (with a wagging finger in the face) "Be a good Christian and do not sin!" or, "*Do* this; *do not* do that!" Why not? Because according to Scripture, they have been given a <u>new</u> heart that naturally *loves* God and *desires* to please Him by keeping His commands, which have been written upon their heart (Ezek.36:26; Heb.8:10)! In other words, because their nature was transformed (down to the core) by faith in Yeshua and their union with Him, a righteous person is *already* effortlessly, naturally, and joyfully living a life that reflects the character of their Father expressed in His Word or laws – and their motivation is LOVE for God, not a sense of moral obligation or duty. As a new creation in Yeshua who shares and reflects His very nature, because our delight and treasure is God *Himself*, without even thinking about it, our lives become an embodiment and reflection of His Word and commands! If we are a believer and God's commands feel heavy or burdensome to us, which 1 John 5:3 says they *shouldn't*, it is simply because we are lacking revelation of our true identity in the Lord and what He accomplished on our behalf.

Think about it: Do you believe Yeshua or Jesus, who *always* did what pleased His Father (John 8:29), had to *think* about keeping His Father's commands and *remind* Himself to live a righteous and obedient life? No - it was just as automatic, natural, and effortless for Him to live righteously as it is for an apple tree to produce apples, or for a fish to breathe under water! If you say, *"Well of course that was true for <u>Jesus</u> because He's the Son of God or God incarnate!"*, remember that He has brought YOU into His life, making you a "slave" to righteousness and a "tree of righteousness" that naturally bears good fruit (Matt.7:18)! This is true for YOU because as He IS, so are YOU in THIS world (1 John 4:17)! This is what Paul meant when he says we do not "need" God's Law or that it isn't "for" *us*, and why the ungodly or wicked DO need it because a distorted identity, condemned conscience, and unrenewed mind keeps them held captive to sin. And until <u>weak believers</u> mature in their revelation of their identity in the Lord and learn to walk by the Spirit, they also *need* God's Law to hold them in check or remind them of what righteous living looks like. This is also what Paul is getting at when he says in Romans 7 that we have "died" to the Law and have been "released" from it. He simply means that once we have been united with Yeshua in His death and resurrection, we *died* <u>not</u> to the Law itself or what it represents, but to its *condemnation* for not perfectly living up to its standards, and we have been released from or have come out from under the *curses* and *judgments* the Law prescribed against us for violating it.

If we misunderstand Paul's writings concerning God's Law, we will make the grave mistake of believing he was *against* God's Law or that he taught it was made obsolete (2 Pet.3:15-16). We also died to living *by* the Law, in the sense that it is not our source of salvation, motivation, righteousness, and spiritual transformation. Our Source is God Himself, and His indwelling Spirit, love, and grace inspire and empower us, *not* His Law. This is the difference between living by the *letter* of the law versus the *spirit* of the law; the former leads to bondage, condemnation, and death, while the latter leads to life, liberty, blessing, and glory! (see Rom.7:6; 2 Cor.3). Obeying God's Law or commandments will *never* bring about *inner* or *spiritual* transformation; only the love of God and His indwelling Spirit can transform our hearts and inspire us to walk in His ways. The main point here is that we must examine the nature of our relationship with God's Word or Law and make sure our motives spring from <u>love</u> and a sincere faith, and that our *joyful* obedience is the fruit of His Spirit in us.

Many Christians "try hard" NOT to sin, and living a holy and obedient life feels difficult and heavy. Why is that? It may be for several reasons, but the primary reason is because they are still relating with Yahweh through the Tree of the Knowledge of Good and Evil, rather than from the Tree of Life, which is Yeshua Himself. What does this mean? We will address this topic again a little later, but it means that if we are not cultivating a *personal* and *living* relationship with the Lord rooted in <u>love</u>, we tend to focus on rules or outward conformity to His commands; we focus more on what WE can *do* rather than what HE <u>did</u> on our behalf. This means that "trying" or striving <u>not</u> to sin is a sin itself. How or why? Because "trying" not to sin is the same as trying to be holy or righteous, which you *cannot* do in your own strength or self-resolve. This is precisely what eating from the Tree of the Knowledge of Good and Evil or living "under the Law" does to you – it puts you on the "hamster wheel" of performance in efforts to obtain what can only be received as a *gift* and by *faith* (see John 6:63; Zech.4:6; Jer.17). We spoke earlier about how this can result in us walking in pride, self-righteousness, and a judgmental, condemning, or critical heart towards others (as the Pharisees did). Or, if we are prone to self-introspection and focus on how much we *fail* to "measure up" to God's standards, it can also lead us in the opposite direction of shame, guilt, and self-condemnation.

This means that partaking of the Tree of the Knowledge of Good and Evil brings us into a "lose-lose" scenario. As with the Law of God, it never imparts *spiritual* life, healing, and freedom, but actually becomes a "ministry of death" and "condemnation" because it focuses on the externals rather than the inward - again, the "letter" or written code of the Law versus the "spirit" of the Law (see 2 Cor.3). However, as Paul also said, because God's Law is holy, righteous, and good, it benefits us greatly if we use it "legally." If we focus on growing in intimacy with the Lord and coming to know His heart and mind, we will *naturally* and *effortlessly* keep His Law because we are "in love"! Yes – love makes it simple *and* a delight, as Yeshua said that HIS yoke is easy and His burden is light, <u>not</u> a wearisome, heavy, and difficult "chore" (Matt.11:28-30)! Just as you will never find a wife who resists or rebels against her husband's *loving, sacrificial,* and *serving* leadership, so we should never find a believer who rebels against their *spiritual* Husband's leadership – that is, if we truly know and trust in His love for us!

When we truly love God, desire His Word, and fear Him, victory over sin, temptation, and disobedience becomes *effortless* because we are doing it in His strength or power. More than that, if the LORD is our Lord or Master, and <u>not</u> His Law, and we share His nature, keeping His laws and resisting sin and temptation isn't something we *do* – it is who we <u>are</u> by our union with Him! It's important to understand that our pursuit of God's kingdom and righteousness in our daily lives is the <u>outward</u> manifestation of the *inner* transformation that took place when we were born-again – that is, *if* in fact we were born-again or made a new creation in Christ. Like Paul said in 1 Corinthians 15:10, we can say God's grace towards us is not *in vain* because it produces in us the desire and power to *labor more abundantly* – yet our labor or fruit does not stem from self-resolve or willpower, but the <u>grace</u> of God in us! (See 2 Cor.7:1; Rom.6; 1 Cor.15:34; 1 Tim.5:20; Heb.10:26,12:14; 1 John). Abiding in Yeshua and entering into His REST is what naturally produces the fruit of His righteousness, love, joy, peace, etc. If we find ourselves striving or toiling to produce this fruit, we must passionately "labor" to enter His rest (see Hebrew chapter 4).

So, by now you should understand that Yahweh never intended for His Law to be our means of meriting our salvation, establishing our own righteousness, or earning His love, acceptance, and favor. Romans 10:2-4 says this was Israel's mistake; they had zeal for God that wasn't rooted in the knowledge of the truth, and they related with the Law as though it was an end in itself. But the Law, which provides moral guidance, was not the end goal, but a means *to* the end goal. Keeping humanity morally in check is definitely important, but that was a *secondary* and *temporary* solution to the *permanent* problem of sin. No matter how great of a job we think we are doing at observing God's Word or laws, our effort or obedience can never take away, expiate, or expunge our sin; neither can it *spiritually* make us clean before God or justify us. Again, as Galatians 2:20-21 says, why would Yeshua need to lay down His life for us if we could secure our salvation or right standing with Yahweh by keeping His commands? While the secondary purpose of the Law is to provide moral guidance for humanity and hold them "in check", the primary or end goal of the Law is twofold:

#1,The Law *reveals* our sin and our spiritually dead state, as Paul said, *I would not have come to know sin except through the Law, for I would not have known about coveting if the Law had not said, "Thou shall not covet,"* and, *by works of the Law no flesh shall be justified in His sight, for through the Law comes knowledge of sin* (Rom.7:7,

3:20). As noted a moment ago, the Law was <u>not</u> given to help us overcome sin and kill it, but to help us see how our sin overcomes *us* and produces condemnation and death, which paves the way to the second purpose of the Law.

#2, The Law *points* or *leads us to* Yeshua, our <u>only</u> remedy or Source of hope, salvation, or redemption! In other words, the Law was given to bring two-fold revelation: revelation of our *sin*, and of our need for the *Savior* or *Messiah*. Galatians 3:23-25 tells us that until we come into a relationship with Him based on faith, the Law acts as our custodian (tutor, manager, or guardian), not only defining righteousness for us, but to help keep us in check morally and warn us of the consequences for violating it (similar to the presence of law enforcement or how the police motivate people to be "law abiding" citizens). Paul says once we come to Yeshua and take on His nature, we "come out from under" this tutor or guardian – <u>not</u> in the sense that our lives no longer need to reflect its righteousness, as many Christians have been led to believe, but that we no longer relate with it as our tutor, principal, or guardian that morally keeps us in line and "cleanses" us by observing it.

What it Means to No Longer be "Under the Law"

As believers, you are not "above the law" just because you are no longer "under" it. What you are no longer under is the penalty of *judgment, condemnation,* and *curse* of the Law (Gal.3:13; Rom.8:24). How or why? Because Yeshua took on or *became* your sin, not only dying FOR you, but AS you. Out of love, He willingly submitted Himself to the Law's demand for judgment and condemnation that *you* rightly deserved! You are also not "under" the law in the sense that you no longer vainly look to it and depend upon it as your <u>source</u> of justification and sanctification, or making yourself presentable and acceptable before God. Now that you are indwelt by the Spirit of God, cleansed by Yeshua's blood and made perfectly righteous before Him by grace through faith alone, you *naturally* and *effortlessly* observe His laws because your source of power and motivation is <u>not</u> the Law itself (e.g., your desire and effort to clean yourself up through outward conformity and performance, duty or obligation). You are not driven or motivated by self-righteous pride, ego, and self-resolve or willpower, but <u>love</u>, <u>passion</u>, and <u>desire</u> by the Holy Spirit! You are empowered by a <u>love relationship</u>, not rules, and because the Law is written on your hearts, you naturally observe the Law.

In reality, you aren't even "keeping" or "observing" the Law, as that implies duty or obligation. Because He has written His laws on your heart and you share His nature, like an internal navigating system, His Word or laws keep and guard YOU. This is the difference between keeping the Law by the *letter* versus the *Spirit* (see Rom.2:29, 7:6). Israel fell into the trap of relating with the Lord through His Law, as though their observance of it became their true source of righteousness, confidence and justification before Him, and that outward conformity alone made them true sons of Abraham. They also believed that being an Israelite, Jew, or a physical descendant of Abraham, automatically made them recipients of God's salvation. But we read in Acts 13:39, *....and by Him* [Yeshua] *everyone who believes is justified from all things which you <u>could not be justified</u> by the law of Moses.* Most Christians have been led to believe that saints who lived before Yeshua came were justified or "saved" by their own righteousness and their observance of God's Law. But that cannot be true because this verse contradicts that belief. If followers of Yahweh were made right with Him by keeping His laws before Christ came, Paul would have said something like, *"Under Moses,* *believers were justified by works or obedience to the Law, but now we are justified by faith in Christ."* But he explicitly says you could <u>not</u> be justified by keeping the laws God gave through Moses. He also wrote in Romans 8:3-4:

For <u>what the Law could not do</u> [make us holy and right before God], *weak as it was through the flesh, <u>GOD</u> did; sending His own Son in the likeness of sinful flesh and as an offering for sin, He condemned sin in the flesh, <u>in order that the requirement of the Law might be fulfilled</u> in us...."*

Paul made this statement in Acts 13:39 and Romans 3 because many who lived before Yeshua came fell into the trap of a justification or salvation-by-works mentality because they falsely concluded that if observing the Law brought *physical* life, protection, and blessing, then it must do likewise *spiritually* – and if following it made them "righteous" in a *physical* or *tangible* sense (Deut.6:25; Lev.18:5), then it must do the same *spiritually*. Apparently, many were still attempting to establish their own righteousness through the Law (and their own laws), even after our Messiah came. This is the default of mankind: to attempt to save or redeem himself and make himself presentable to God, to merit His love, approval, and favor through his own efforts and goodness. But this is antithetical to the Gospel and the Scriptures! Hebrews 11 makes it clear that all the saints who lived before Yeshua "gained approval" or "obtained a good testimony" <u>not</u> by their law-keeping, but by their FAITH, which <u>resulted</u> in obedience to Yahweh's laws, as Romans 4:2 says, *Abraham believed God* [or had faith], *and it was reckoned* [credited] *to him as righteousness;* and Romans 16:26 speaks of the "obedience of faith." However, Hebrews 3:15-19 tells us that the reason many did not make it into the Promised Land or inherit God's promises was because of their <u>unbelief</u> or <u>lack of faith</u>, which *led* to their disobedience. And we read in Hebrews 4:2:

For we also have had the gospel preached to us, just as they did, but the word they heard did <u>not</u> profit them because it was <u>not</u> united by <u>faith</u> in those who heard.

If Old Testament saints were redeemed, saved, or justified by law-keeping, why would it be any different for us, and why would Yeshua need to give His life? As noted earlier, Galatians 2:21 says, *if righteousness could be attained by Law, then Christ died needlessly.* Paul also says <u>no one</u> *is justified by the Law in the sight of God, 'for the righteous shall live by his <u>faith</u>,'* and, *those who are of <u>faith</u> are sons of Abraham,* and, *that the blessing of Abraham might come upon the Gentiles in Christ, that we might receive the promise of the Spirit through <u>faith</u>* (see Galatians ch.3). The truth is, throughout history, *anyone* who attempts to redeem, justify, and sanctify themselves by keeping the Law is living "under the Law" in the sense that they fall under its judgment and will be condemned by it. If you depend upon the Law or your disciplined observance of it as your source of justification or righteousness before Yahweh, it will judge, incriminate, and condemn you – *without* mercy. In other words, if you think, *"I'll do my best to keep God's laws to avoid sin,"* you are not only trusting in your self-resolve and own strength, but you are also living "under" and "by" the Law in a way God never intended!

More than that, you are under a "spell" or delusion, as Paul said to the Galatians, because you apparently believe that YOU, by your own works or performance, can earn and deserve what can only come by way of <u>faith</u> in Yeshua and HIS work. As the principle is true that "if you live by the sword, you will die by the sword," so it is true that if you live by the Law, where your confidence before God is rooted in *yourself* or your own performance rather than <u>Yeshua's</u> finished and perfect work, you will *die* by it because the LAW will be your Judge, not God (and the Law will show no mercy!). As we already discussed, this is what Paul was getting at when he said the Law, which is holy, righteous, and good, can become a ministry of *death* and *condemnation* when we use it in a way God did not intend.

While keeping His Law will serve us well by mitigating the damage caused by sin, or protecting and preserving our lives in a *physical* sense, it makes a terrible master when we wrongly use it as a means of gaining *spiritual* life and our justification before God. When we use it "legally" as Yahweh intended, where we fully trust *Yeshua* as our Master and Savior, with His love, grace, and Spirit as our source of motivation and power, the Law finds its proper place in our life and serves us very well (1 Tim.1:8)! Paul did not call the Law "spiritual" in Romans 7:14 because our observance of it redeems us or because it creates faith within us. He said it is spiritual simply because God is its Author or because it came from heaven, and because it opens our spiritual eyes to see our sin and it prepares our heart or spirit to receive Yeshua as our Savior. But he clearly says the Law is "<u>not</u> based on faith" (Gal.3:12). How can the Law of God be "spiritual" and yet not based on faith? Because it does not require "faith" to believe that keeping God's Law will *physically* preserve and bless our lives– as there is an obvious correlation between cause and effect or sowing and reaping.

Didn't God clearly say that *if* His people kept His Law, *then* He would bless them? Do we really believe God "blesses" disobedience or loose living or an abuse of His grace? What earthly parent would pour blessing and favor onto a child who was characterized as rebellious and disobedient? We're not talking about whether or not God still *loves* us if we're walking in disobedience – this is about walking in His favor and blessings. And we aren't talking about placing faith in OUR obedience or righteousness to experience God's favor and blessings – nor faith in our faith; this is about the faith of God given to us as a gift and about resting in the finished work of YESHUA that not only brings His blessing into our lives, but produces His character and the fruit of righteousness and obedience (as Rom.1:5;16:25 speak of the "obedience of faith").

"But the Bible says Jesus is the END of the Law!"

We read in Romans 10:3-4 and Galatians 3:10-12:

For not knowing about God's righteousness, and seeking to establish their own, they [Israel] *did not subject themselves to the righteousness of God, <u>for Christ is the end of the Law</u> for <u>righteousness</u> for everyone who believes. For Moses writes that the man who practices the righteousness which is based on law shall live* [physically] *by that righteousness.*

For all who rely on the works of the law are under a curse, for it is written: CURSED IS EVERYONE WHO DOES NOT ABIDE BY ALL THINGS WRITTEN IN THE BOOK OF THE LAW, TO PERFORM THEM. Now it is clear that no one is justified before God by the Law, because the righteous man shall live by <u>faith</u>. But the Law is <u>not</u> based on faith; instead, the one who does these things shall live [physically] *by them.*

Sadly, many Christians read such passages (out of context) and conclude that Christ ENDED the Law of God and that if we endeavor to *keep* His commands, it places us under a curse! Keeping the Law <u>does</u> place us under a curse if we're doing it in efforts to sanctify ourselves and obtain salvation, and this is what Paul is saying in Galatians. He is <u>not</u> saying Christ ended the Law, but that Christ is the end of the Law FOR RIGHTEOUSNESS <u>*for everyone who believes*</u>. Again, CONTEXT is everything - in this case, just reading the *rest of the sentence* and *next verse!* Reading verse 3 without verse 4 makes a huge difference in our understanding of what Paul is trying to communicate. This is in *addition* to understanding the original language. The Greek word for "end" is *telos*, which means *"to set out for a definite point, goal or purpose."* This means Yeshua represents the *goal* or *purpose* of the Law, which begs the question: <u>what</u> goal or purpose? As we have seen, one purpose of the Law is to expose our sin as we are guilty of falling terribly short of its demands, and because Yeshua is the Word incarnate, we are looking at *Him* and His perfect character or nature when we look into His Law. Yeshua's purpose in His flawless observance of the Law is to point us to *Himself,* our perfect example of righteousness and only source of salvation. The Law points to Him, saying, "<u>This</u> is what righteousness looks like," the living Word who perfectly kept the Law, thus being qualified to make atonement for our sins, cleanse our guilty conscience, and make us righteous (2 Cor.5:21). Once we are joined to Him and share in His righteousness and nature, He empowers us by His Spirit to *physically* manifest that righteousness by following in His footsteps – fleshing out the Law as a natural result, not trivializing or discarding it. If we understand Paul's point here, even if the words, "for righteousness," were not in this verse, Yeshua is still the end *goal* or *purpose* of the Law for believers.

If Paul was saying Jesus brought an "end" to the Law in that He nullified it, that would not only imply that getting rid of the Law was a *good* thing, but Paul would be contradicting himself. For instance, he says our faith *establishes* or *affirms* the Law and that the Law is *spiritual, holy, righteous and good;* he *joyfully agreed* with it, walked according to the Law, and said that those who do *not* submit to the Law are *carnal* or *fleshly* and *hostile* towards Yahweh (Rom.3:31, 7:12,14, 8:5-8, Acts 21:24).[20] Peter also uses the Greek word, *telos,* in I Peter 1:9 when he speaks of *obtaining the outcome (telos) of our faith, the salvation of our souls.* Peter is <u>not</u> saying our faith comes to an "end" when we come to Yeshua, but that the *point, goal or purpose* of our faith is the <u>salvation</u> of our souls. Paul uses the word, *telos,* in Romans 6:22 as well. It says, *But now that you have been set free from sin and have become slaves of God, the fruit you get leads to sanctification and its end [telos], eternal life.* Is he saying holiness will come to a halt or that our eternal life will one day come to an end? Of course not!

Another common interpretation of this verse is that Christ brought an end to our need to attain righteousness through keeping Yahweh's Law – as many mistakenly believe Old Testaments saints lived under the "Age of Law" and had to attain their righteousness before Yahweh through law-keeping. This is assumed because Paul writes in the very next verse: *"since Moses writes about the righteousness that is from the law: the one who does these things shall live by them."* Deuteronomy 6:25 also says, *"if we are careful to obey all this law before Yahweh, as He has commanded, that will be our righteousness."* We say, *"See – it's right there – Old Testament saints were made righteous through law-keeping!"* But no, NO person, at *any* time in history can be justified, made right, perfect, holy and acceptable before Yahweh through keeping His Law! Even some of the Old Testament saints had this revelation or understanding, as Habakkuk 2:4 says, *the righteous shall live by faith* (not Law). If we could attain perfection through the Law, then the Bible contradicts itself. How could the Law make us right with God *before* Yeshua came, but not *after* He came? While we can't attain a perfect or truly right standing before God by keeping His Law, we *can* reflect the righteousness of His Law by living or fleshing it out. Just because we cannot do so *perfectly* does <u>not</u> mean we cannot be called righteous or holy (e.g., Gen.6:9, Job 1:1, Acts 10:22). But the righteousness we need *for salvation* and reconciliation with Yahweh is something we can <u>never</u> attain by our own efforts of keeping the Law, as again, we would have to do it flawlessly as Yeshua did. This is Paul's point in Romans 10, when he says Israel's fatal error that we should not repeat was attempting to establish their *own* righteousness or perfection through law-keeping, rather than through faith. Whether they are

God's or man's, laws can never be used as a means of *perfecting* ourselves before God. Romans 8:3-4 says: *For what the <u>Law could not do</u>, weak as it was through the flesh, <u>God did</u>: sending His own <u>Son</u> in the likeness of sinful flesh and as an offering for sin, He condemned sin in the flesh, <u>so that the requirement of the Law might be fulfilled in us</u>.*

What was it that the Law could not do and why? Because of the weakness of our sin nature and condemned conscience, it could not make us perfect before God or made right with Him. What did Yahweh do? He took on human likeness in Yeshua, obeying the Law *flawlessly,* becoming a guilt offering for our sin. The result was that the Law's demand of <u>perfect righteousness</u> and the curses which come upon us for breaking it were fulfilled in all who trust in Him! The result of this gift of grace is that we *naturally* desire to live out our faith by doing what pleases our Lord: obeying His commands – allowing Yeshua to be our *example*, not our *excuse* for *not* keeping His Word. Whether a person lived *before* Yeshua or *after*, we can all fall into the trap of trying to earn salvation or establishing our own righteousness (e.g., Rom.10:3). But once we understand we are declared right before God by grace through faith alone, it does not negate His command for us to practically walk out that righteousness which His law defines. If we allow His grace to lull us into passivity towards the righteous living His Law commands, we have received His grace in vain, because it empowers us to love Him by naturally and joyfully *keeping* His laws, showing the world what righteousness looks like, and the liberty, blessing and peace that comes from walking in His ways (See Mark 8:34/ John 12:22 / Rom.3:31 / I Cor.6:17, 11:1 / Gal.5:16 / Phil.2:12-13 / I John 2:6).

Let's look at Paul again. Paul said he had every reason (before man) to boast in the righteousness he had that was based on his observance of God's Law, but he gladly gave up his boasting and self-reliance because he wanted to be solely found in *Yeshua*, <u>not</u> having a righteousness of his own that was derived from law-keeping, but that which is through faith in HIM – the righteousness that comes from GOD on the basis of FAITH, not works (Phil.3:9). Unless we are "towing the line" perfectly like Yeshua did, the righteousness we can have through keeping God's laws is not only physical, practical, and visible, but totally *imperfect* as far as He is concerned, but the *perfect* or *spotless* righteousness we need for justification and reconciliation with God comes by <u>faith</u> in Yeshua and His sacrifice *alone*! Pardon the redundancy, but hopefully you are beginning to understand how important it is that we *rightly* relate with God's Law and approach His commands through faith and love (rather than self-trust/effort and a sense of religious duty or obligation). It is important to note that James 2:20 does <u>not</u> say faith, in and of itself, IS our works or obedience, but that faith *without* works is dead. But how can we be sure our faith is genuine or that our works are truly pleasing to the Lord? Our faith and obedience must be the *overflow* of a <u>love relationship</u> with the Lord, as Galatians 5:6b and 1 Timothy 1:5 say: *Faith works through <u>love</u>; The goal of our instruction is <u>love</u> from a pure heart and a good conscience and a sincere <u>faith</u>.* And we remember the Lord's words in John 14:5, *"If you <u>love</u> Me, you will keep My commands."*

In summary, if our love and faith are a fruit of God's Spirit, they will naturally express themselves through joyful <u>obedience</u> to God's Law and manifest a life of effortless <u>victory</u> over sin and temptation - a life that demonstrates the righteousness and power of Yeshua! And again, it is vital to understand that if our source of power and motivation is our flesh or self-resolve, and if the Law itself is our Master, Guardian, or Tutor, living in obedience to God's laws and walking in victory over sin and temptation will *never* be "natural," joyful, and effortless. Believers who are law or duty-driven, and therefore take pride in their moral superiority, are very unhappy and judgmental people. If we are truly resting in the finished work of Yeshua and are cultivating a relationship with Him rooted in faith and empowered by His love and grace, we will be a people of joy, peace, and rest because it is the Spirit of Yeshua <u>in</u> us which naturally produces the fruit as we abide in Him. We are also at rest because we no longer have to defend and justify ourselves before others because we know we are *already* righteous and perfect before God in Yeshua! Just as spouses who truly love one another have ZERO struggles with resisting temptation because there is absolutely NO desire to sin against one another (including God and themselves), so we as God's people will *effortlessly* and *naturally* say no to sin when we truly love *Him* and know His love for *us*! The Good News of the Gospel really is *that* good!

For Christ's love fuels our passion and motivates us, because we are convinced that He has given His life for all of us. This means all died with Him... 2 Cor.5:14-15 TPT

Could it not be any clearer that our former identity is now and forever deprived of its power? For we were co-crucified with Him to dismantle the stronghold of sin within us, so that we would not continue to live one moment longer submitted to sin's power, for obviously, a dead person is incapable of sinning. Rom.6:6-7 TPT

Some believe mixing law with grace will make a "deadly concoction." This is true – that is, IF we mix self-righteous law-keeping in efforts to *earn* salvation and God's love with His *unconditional, unmerited* love and grace through the perfect and complete work of Yeshua. Again, this is precisely what the believers in Galatia did. And have you ever noticed that Paul was more upset with the well-behaved Galatians than he was with the believers in Corinth, who had gross sins of immorality in their ranks? How is that possible? Paul certainly believed that *abusing* God's grace through willful sin is heinous, as he addressed that issue in Romans chapter six, but nothing made him angrier than a *rejection* of God's grace or the attempt to *improve* upon it through our own performance or law-keeping! Paul made it clear that we are not redeemed, sanctified, and physically healed by the blood of Yeshua and the grace of God PLUS our fleshly efforts to make ourselves presentable to God through keeping His Law. However, as we have already noted, he also made it clear that God's love and grace do not cancel out our obedience to His commands, rather they *constrain, compel, inspire,* and *empower* us to live free from sin and joyfully (and effortlessly) live according to His ways (Rom.2:12, 3:31, 7:7-12). The question is, what is our *motive* and what is our *source of power* and *inspiration?* The following pages contain a simple comparison chart that may help us understand the difference between living "under the law" and grace.

LIVING "UNDER"/BY <u>LAW</u>
(Tree of Knowledge of Good & Evil)

<u>Master/"Savior"/ Tutor</u>: God's Law (Letter of the Law)

<u>Power Source</u>: *Flesh or Natural Man* (self-resolve & discipline). Try to kill the flesh BY the flesh; God's Law or the Bible is treated like a "self-help" manual (Gal.2; Rom.10)

<u>Focus</u>: LAW & SELF: Focus on their good performance, leading to pride & self-righteousness, OR Focus on their poor performance & sin, leading to shame & condemnation.

<u>Motive</u>: *Duty/Obligation: to boost ego, to look good/right.* Try to merit God's love & favor through performance. Fear rejection & punishment. May truly desire to please God, but try to do so through their own works. Live FOR God, not FROM God. Aim = to conform to LAW & highlight *their* goodness, not Yeshua's.

<u>Traits</u>: *Prideful/Self-righteous*: "I'm doing great! Thank God I'm not like those sinful pagans or worldly Christians!" **OR** *Guilt & Condemnation*: "I'm such a sinner - I never measure up!"

<u>Result</u>: False humility, No true joy/peace, Defensive, Unteachable **OR** Self-condemning, Victim mentality; In bondage because they relate with God through His Law rather than grace, love, & intimacy. No rest, but toil to rely on the flesh to obtain what was freely given by grace through faith in the finished work of Yeshua. Weary from establishing/defending their "own" righteousness.

Based on the LIE: **Faith + Works = Salvation** (Faith & Obedience OBTAINS & SECURES Salvation)

LIVING UNDER/BY <u>GRACE</u>
(Tree of Life)

<u>**Master/Savior/Teacher/Shepherd**</u>: Yeshua (Spirit of the Law)

<u>**Power Source**</u>: *Holy Spirit and Grace* (Phil.2:13,4:13; Col.2:29;Titus 2:11-12)

<u>**Focus**</u>: <u>Yeshua</u> & <u>His</u> righteousness IN them

<u>**Motive**</u>: *Love & Desire, & to glorify GOD, making HIM look good!* Relationship-driven & Pursuit of Intimacy (2 Cor.5:14; John 14:5; 1 John 5:3; Gal.5:6b; 1 Tim.1:5; 2 Cor.5:14). Live FROM God, not FOR Him. Aim = conform to YESHUA & reflect <u>His</u> goodness, not theirs.

<u>**Traits**</u>: *Humble, Teachable, Approachable:* Know the true righteousness Yahweh accepts is by grace through faith in YESHUA alone; *Peace, Joy, Rest.*

<u>**Result**</u>: Observe God's laws out of <u>love</u> & by the <u>Spirit</u>, rather than the letter & by the flesh or self-resolve. Walk in true FREEDOM because they know their identity & acceptance is found Yeshua alone & HIS finished work; This liberty in the Lord's finished work effortlessly produces the fruit of obedience, godliness & Christ-likeness.

Based on the TRUTH: **Faith = Salvation + Work** (Faith Alone Provides the GIFT of Salvation, naturally producing the Fruit of Holiness & Obedience)

When the Bible Becomes an Idol

As David expressed in the Psalms, we should *love* the Word of God or Scriptures because our heavenly Father is the Author, who's words bring guidance, life, and blessing to our flesh. Many would say we can't idolize the Bible because it ultimately comes from Him, but many believers do it. Isn't it possible to cherish or love the *gift* more than the Giver? As noted, it is possible for us to know the *written* Word of God or the Bible from cover to cover <u>without</u> knowing the *Living* Word of God (Yeshua). Growing in our knowledge of God and His Word is vital and we should always be studying to "show ourselves approved," but we should not assume that being a Bible expert or having a seminary degree means all of our doctrine is sound and or that we have an intimate and healthy relationship with the Lord. Nor does it mean that those who lack formal training or higher education are more likely to be wrong in their doctrine and immature in their walk with God. Consider the disciples whom Yeshua chose, as Acts 4:13 says:

Now as they [Pharisees] *observed the confidence of Peter and John, and understood that they were uneducated and untrained men, they marveled, and began to recognize that <u>they had been with Jesus</u>.*

In other words, *relationship* or *intimacy* was the key – and it forever will be! We cannot be so focused on theology, doctrine, or God's laws or commandments that we allow the Word of God to keep us from encountering <u>God</u> of the Word. The Bible is <u>not</u> a mere religious textbook, rather it is the *living* and *active* Word of God. Of course, we should strive for sound doctrine and be committed to knowing and memorizing Scripture, as it provides the foundation of our faith, but the Bible is not an invitation to theological knowledge or a manual on behavioral modification through rule-keeping. This is why you may have heard that Bible colleges or seminaries are becoming more like "cemeteries" because for many, academia, head knowledge and doctrinal debate have been pursued at the expense of a living faith and experiential knowledge of God. In other words, some find more satisfaction in theology and impressing others with *what* they know over *who* they know and proving themselves *right* over proving the *will* and *word* of God (Rom.12:2; Acts 14:3).

Again, the Bible or the Word of God is a divine invitation to *relationship* and *transformation*, which only happens when His Word goes beyond information to revelation, where out of intimacy with Yahweh, we become conformed into the image of Yeshua, as His nature, kingdom, and will are increasingly manifested in our lives. Of course, we *cannot* have revelation without information, but we can indeed have information without revelation – just as we *cannot* truly love God without observing His laws, but we can observe His laws without loving or even knowing Him. But what exactly is "revelation"? We receive revelation when the truth of Yahweh's Word goes beyond our intellect and into our spirit man, where it becomes alive to us and becomes a part of our very "spiritual DNA," transforming our lives from the inside out. We know the Word says that when we are born-again, Yahweh *regenerates* us; the Lord literally, not just doctrinally or figuratively, "re-GENE-erates" our spiritual DNA or genetic makeup, truly making us a "new" creature who is no longer bound to behave as ordinary, "mere men" (Titus 3:5; 1 Cor.3:3). In order for us to truly undergo transformation through revelation, it cannot be second-hand, where someone else shares with us revelation *they* have received. We can certainly glean exciting insights that way and our lives can be impacted to some degree, but revelation which brings true and lasting transformation must come to us *personally* as a result of our *own* pursuit of God and our intimacy with Him.

Concerning knowledge alone, His Word tells us that "knowledge puffs up," where we can be "ever learning without coming to the knowledge of truth" and having a zeal for God that is not based on true knowledge (1 Cor.8:1; 2 Tim.3:7; Rom.10:2). There are many benefits to formal training or higher education, and we thank the Lord for the scholars He has raised up throughout the generations who have made tremendous contributions to the Body (and to the *world,* helping unbelievers and seekers of truth to overcome intellectual hurdles through the study of apologetics). But we must be careful to avoid the trap of placing confidence in our *knowledge, accomplishments, degrees,* or *accolades* over knowing the Lord Himself in a personal and living way. Yeshua said in Luke 16:15:

"You are those who justify yourselves in the sight of men, but God knows your heart; for that which is highly esteemed among men is detestable in the sight of God."

Yahweh is obviously not against education or higher learning, for He commands us to love Him with all our heart <u>and</u> *minds,* and once he was transformed, Paul's advanced education was used greatly by God to build up the Church, win converts, and make disciples. But ultimately, it is about WHO we know, not *what* we know, and in whom we place our confidence - not in ourselves or our intellect, but *Him* (Paul talks about this in Philippians chapter 3). Before Paul became known to the Church, his goal in life was not only to know the *written* Word of God or Scriptures, namely, the Torah (the first 5 books of the Bible) and the Prophets, but especially the *traditions of the elders* (laws and ordinances that were *added* to the Torah by the religious leaders of his day). Thankfully that totally changed for him after his encounter with Yeshua. In spite of all his knowledge, experience, and impact, Paul said he pressed towards the goal of <u>*knowing*</u> *Yeshua.* He had spent his previous life feeding on the *manna* of God for physical life, guidance, and blessing, but "missed the forest for the trees," not understanding that true <u>spiritual</u> life does not come from the "letter of the Law," and especially not from the traditions and doctrines of man, but only through cultivating intimacy with *Yeshua*, the *Living* Word, the Messiah and true Bread of Life whom Yahweh revealed to the world! As Yeshua said:

"You study the Scriptures diligently because you think that in them you have eternal life; these are the very Scriptures which testify about Me, yet you refuse to come to <u>Me</u> that you may have this life." John 5:39-40

"Very truly I tell you, it is <u>not</u> Moses who has given you the bread from heaven, but it is My Father who gives you the true bread from heaven. For the bread of God is the bread that comes down from heaven and gives life to the world.......I Am the Bread of Life. Your fathers ate the bread in the wilderness and died. But here is the Bread that comes down from heaven. Whoever eats this Bread will live forever. This Bread is My flesh, which I will give for the life of the world;.....My flesh is true food and My blood is true drink." John 6:32-33,48-51

Yeshua clearly tells us that the Word given through Moses (the Law of God) is <u>not</u> the Bread of heaven and *true* spiritual food and drink. As noted a moment ago, the Bible tells us that observing the written Word of God (the Law and Prophets) brings *physical* life and blessing, and can make us *physically* or *practically* righteous. However, the Lord gave His Law as a *means* to an end – not as the end itself. We cannot find eternal or spiritual life in the Law of God or His Word itself; it merely POINTS us to the true end or our true goal and prize: Yeshua, who Romans 10:4 says is the end or goal of the Law (as He perfectly lived out the Law and reflects its righteousness), as well as an living, intimate knowledge and relationship with our heavenly Father, and *out of that intimacy,* giving the world a picture of what the Father looks like as we walk in the righteousness of His ways and destroy the works of Satan in the power of His Spirit![21]

If the laws of God or the Scriptures were all we needed for spiritual life and salvation, would it not have been pointless (to say the least) for Yeshua to sacrifice Himself? This is why it is important to understand that knowledge is to the *mind* what revelation is to the *spirit*. This means Yeshua's true identity must be *revealed* to our inner man <u>before</u> He can be "received" and known in our spirit. When Peter confessed Yeshua to be the true Messiah and Son of God in Matthew 16, Yeshua said to him, *"Blessed are you Simon Barjona, because flesh and blood did not reveal this to you, but My <u>Father</u> who is in heaven."* In other words, Yeshua was saying Peter couldn't take credit for "catching" the revelation of His true identity. The Spirit of GOD is the One who opens our eyes to see Yeshua as He truly is, as Paul affirms in 1 Corinthians 12:3, *no one can say "Yeshua is Lord" <u>except</u> by the Holy Spirit,* and Yeshua said in John chapter 6, *"No one can come to Me <u>unless</u> the <u>Father</u> who sent Me draws him...everyone who has heard and learned <u>from the Father</u>, comes to Me; no one can come to Me unless it has been granted him from the Father"* and Luke 10:22b, *"No one knows the Son except the Father, and no one knows the Father except the Son, and <u>anyone whom the Son wills to reveal Him</u>."*

Remember: Knowledge is to the <u>mind</u> what revelation is to the <u>spirit</u>, meaning Yeshua must <u>reveal</u> Himself to us before we can truly <u>receive</u> & <u>know</u> Him.

CHAPTER 8

How the Natural & Spiritual Work Together

Thanks to advances and discoveries in the fields of science, biology, and physiology, humankind has abandoned the false notion that the unseen realm has nothing to do with the visible realm. The more study, exploration, and research is conducted, the more we learn how the spiritual world greatly affects the natural world. One of the most profound and life-altering discoveries involves the connection between the mind and body, or how our thoughts and beliefs (the immaterial) influence not only our body, but our everyday life (the material). Most of us understand that one facet of being fashioned in God's image or likeness is that we are tri-part beings. God is one Being, yet He is known and exists as Father, Son, and Spirit. Likewise, we are one being, comprised of spirit, soul, and body. Our soul, which is our mind, will, and emotions, expresses itself through our thoughts, desires, and feelings, while our spirit expresses itself through our core convictions and beliefs. All of these things - how we think, how we emotionally feel, and what we inwardly believe about ourselves, come together to form actions and habits in our lives that create our state of being, way of living, and personality.

We briefly touched on this earlier, but this means our heart and mind arrive at our destination before our life does. In short, what we *believe* about ourselves and what we *declare* over ourselves creates our reality or determines *what* we are, *where* we are, *who* we are, and what we *do* ("declaring" something over ourselves simply refers to "self-talk" or the inner dialogue we all have with ourselves daily). Life teaches us that what we feel and believe we <u>are</u> always dominates what we feel and believe we <u>desire </u>to be, and that confessions which begin with, "I <u>am</u>," overpower or dominate those which begin with,

"I am <u>not</u>." While our experiences can surely impact us negatively, we are <u>not</u> helpless victims of our external reality or environment. If we are joined to Yeshua, we are "more than conquerors" or *absolute victors,* and being a "victim" should be *impossible* because we are fashioned in the image of Yahweh, share in His divine nature, and are commanded (and empowered by His Spirit) to emulate or imitate Him. We say it "should" be impossible because as His sons, God has given *us* the power to decide whether or not our circumstances mold us into anything less than the image of His Son. He has given *us* the choice of whether or not we give Satan a foothold in our lives, and as the gatekeepers of our minds, He has given *us* the freedom to think, dwell, or meditate[22] on whatever we desire – even if it opposes or conflicts with *His* Word, thoughts, or declarations about us. Just like our relationships with people, the enemy cannot discourage, frustrate, or anger us and cause us to sin *without* our consent and cooperation.

But due to false teaching concerning the relationship between God's sovereignty and our free will, untold damage has been caused in the lives of millions of believers. God is indeed "sovereign," but that does not mean He orchestrates or controls every event in our lives or coerces us to carry out His will. **He has obligated Himself to fulfill His *promises* in our lives, but <u>not</u> to fulfill *our potential* and *destiny.*** Why? It may sound obvious, but because God's promises are *His*, and our potential and destiny is *ours*. As Lamentations 1:9 says, because Israel *"did not consider her destiny, her collapse was awesome."* Israel did not collapse or go into exile because Yahweh willed it so, but because She did not know (or had lost) Her true identity and purpose. Thankfully, the Holy Spirit is with us to guide and empower us, but whether or not we walk in obedience and fulfill His purpose for our lives is <u>our</u> choice alone! The Bible clearly teaches that through the faith God has given us, WE are responsible to fulfill our potential and walk out our destiny. The Lord will surely fulfill

His promise to give us the courage and strength to do so, and will lead or guide us by His Spirit, but it is up to *us* whether or not we will exercise our faith through obedience and action. Do not miss this; read it several times if needed, because if this truth becomes a revelation for you and you begin to *apply* it, your life will never be the same! I emphasize the word "apply," because contrary to popular belief, knowledge itself is not power; knowledge *rightly applied* is power (and wisdom). We must understand this powerful truth:

Without knowing it, all false doctrines and beliefs we embrace will create a false sense of identity, which lead us into various forms of captivity and cause our life to align or agree with those false, inner core convictions.

Let me elaborate to help you absorb this. As we have seen, Proverbs 23:7 says *as a man thinks in his <u>heart</u>* [inner convictions], *so <u>is</u> he* [physically or outwardly].[23] Because thoughts and words are like seeds, whatever we inwardly believe and focus upon will eventually manifest itself in our everyday lives in some form or another. We could also say that whatever we allow and tolerate in our lives will dominate, be it sickness, lack, fear, depression, etc. As 2 Peter 2:19 says, a man is *enslaved* or *controlled* by what overcomes or dominates him. This means that our spirit, presence, or "shadow" will emanate or release whatever *overshadows* <u>us</u> and leaves not only an impression on us, but also on those around us. In other words, ***all outward <u>expressions</u> are ultimately a manifestation of inward <u>impressions</u>,*** and as Yeshua said in Mark 16, "signs and wonders" do not lead or precede, but <u>follow</u> those who believe (because signs are *seen*, while beliefs are *unseen*). Depending on what is transpiring within us, this could be a good *or* a bad thing. When you hear someone say a person has good or bad "vibes," they are simply referring to that person's positive or negative vibrations, energy, or presence. Even when we don't visually see them, are there not times when we physically *sensed* a person's energy, presence, or mood when they walked into the room or quietly approached us from behind? We are spirit beings housed in a body, which is why we talk about someone "having eyes in the back of their head" or having 6th sense. If radio waves and certain sound waves or pitches are undetectable to the human eye and ear without a receiver, and yet we know they exist and are real, why could this not be true concerning unseen vibrations or waves of energy that we carry, radiate, or emit?

Science <u>proves</u> that our bodies are primarily energy in motion, [24] vibrating at a very high frequency, and that the healthier or more positive our inner thoughts and beliefs are, the higher the frequency we emit or emanate. Most Christians immediately shut their ears to such facts, thinking that because unbelievers use such terminology and have learned to benefit from such knowledge, it must be falsehood based on "New Age" or demonic ideology. This is precisely what some people thought when the radio and television were invented – labeling them witchcraft, black magic, or sorcery. As they say, we reject and mock what we do not know or that for which we have no "grid." Some truths may feel "new" to us when we discover them, but there is nothing "new" about this; science, biology, and physiology affirm that Yahweh "wired" us this way and validate how He created the material world.

More believers are coming to understand that science or the natural world do not conflict with faith or the spirit realm. How could they, considering Hebrews 11:3 emphatically tells us that everything we see in the natural/temporal realm *came out of* the spiritual/eternal realm? (2 Cor.4:18)[25] Didn't God say in Genesis 1:31 that <u>everything</u> He created is "very good"? As long as such fields of study are not used to confirm our biases or to falsify paradigms we disagree with, they are our *friend* and *servant*, not our enemy! If the Bible was written today, some of the authors would have surely used scientific language to teach how the spiritual and physical (or faith and science) work together, but they lived long before advances in technology or scientific research and discovery would have allowed them to do so. They didn't even have the vocabulary or terminology at that time. Obviously, the Lord has forever known these truths because He established them, but He spoke to the writers (and us, the audience) in a language they understood and filtered it through the lens of their limited knowledge and worldview. Besides this, revelation is progressive in nature, as Yeshua gives us finite humans "crumbs" of insight or revelation as we move from one level of glory to another in our faith. We are already *sons,* and the world is waiting for us to manifest our sonship and the glory we carry in Yeshua. And this manifestation is not to be seen as a "work," but something that is to be an effortless byproduct of our faith and fixing our gaze on Him (see 2 Cor.3:18). Colossians 2:3 also says that in Him are "hidden all the treasures of wisdom and knowledge." If He didn't teach us line upon line and precept upon precept, but revealed everything to us at once, to say we wouldn't be able to comprehend and process it or know how to apply it to our lives would be a gross understatement. As Yeshua told His disciples, *"I have <u>much more</u> to say to you, <u>but you cannot bear</u>* [handle] *<u>it now</u>, but when He, the Spirit of truth comes, <u>He will guide into all the truth</u>; He <u>will</u> teach you <u>all things</u>"* (John 16:12-13, 14:26). These statements clearly imply that as history unfolds, the Holy Spirit will reveal truths to His Bride that She has not yet heard or learned. Considering Isaiah 9:7 says the increase of God's kingdom or government will *never* end, along with the fact that God is *infinite* in wisdom, glory, power, holiness, etc., how could this <u>not</u> be?[26] Isn't it exciting to know that we will *forever* be learning about the glory of our great God and His kingdom – and more importantly, how to practically or tangibly flesh it out?

The Scriptures *do* make a clear connection between spirit and body, as again, Proverbs 23:7 says we *are* what we *believe* we are. This obviously does not mean a person can change their ethnicity, age, gender, or species simply by *believing* it! When Yeshua said "all things" are possible, He clearly meant all things which do not violate logic or God's Word and will. As human beings, we were created in the image and likeness of *God*, not animals or plants, and He made male and female as distinct and separate persons or genders within their specific nationality and skin color. If we are in Yeshua, Ephesians chapter 4 says that if we are to fully "lay aside" the old sinful self, we must be *renewed* in the spirit of our *minds,* and put on the *new self, which was <u>created to be like God</u> in true righteousness and holiness.* Did you catch that? *You were created to be like God!* If that sounds offensive, remember that being "like God" is exactly what it means to be "godly." And Paul goes on to say in chapter 5 that we are *commanded* to <u>imitate</u> God. Of course, we are not God, nor will we ever *become* God, as some false religions teach, but as those who are fashioned in His image and indwelt by His presence, we share in His nature, which means by the power of His Spirit, we can imitate or emulate Him! Because we are vessels or conduits of energy and presence (either good/evil or positive/negative), the only way we can live in righteousness, peace, and joy, we must learn to constantly abide in Yeshua and "dwell under the shadow of the Almighty" (Rom.14:17; Ps.91). Paul writes in 2 Corinthians 3:18:

But we all, with unveiled face, beholding as in a mirror the glory of the Lord, are being transformed <u>into the same image</u> from glory to glory.

In other words, we manifest or become like that which we behold or focus upon. We just touched on this, but this means the physical or external (our energy/choices/actions) naturally flow out of and reflect whatever we focus upon internally or spiritually (our hearts, minds, and beliefs). We could also say it this way: ***whatever*** *we focus on, we will connect with; whatever we become conscious of, we become occupied with, and whatever we become occupied with will dominate or rule our lives.* This isn't some "New Age" principle – it's simply how God wired us. Isn't this what Paul is saying when it comes to our relationship with the Lord? He's saying that if we gaze at Yeshua with the eyes of our hearts and set our affection and attention upon Him, our lives will increasingly attract and reflect His glory, and we tangibly become more like Him! Yes, we are already like Him spiritually (our spirit-man), but our soul and body have a lot of "catching up" to do, so to speak! This is where the "fight" comes in, as we learn to physically and outwardly manifest who we <u>already are</u> spiritually and internally. The point is, to the degree that we focus on Yeshua and meditate on our union with Him, to that same degree will our physical/tangible lives manifest His image/likeness!

Does this mean we can come to the place where we literally and perpetually walk in perfection like Yeshua did, <u>never</u> grieving or quenching His Spirit by having ungodly thoughts, actions, or impure motives, etc.? That is surely in the realm of possibility, as the Lord said in Mark 9:23, "*all things* are possible to him who believes," but aside from our Messiah, has any person throughout history ever done that from the time they were born-again? When we speak of a "sin-free" life, we mean violating God's Word or laws is extremely rare for us, not routine and intentional as it is for sinners or so many professing "believers." We are talking about living a life where sinful or fleshly behavioral and thought patterns and habits no longer have a hold on us and we have experienced victory over that which had dominion over us – whether it's impatience, unrighteous anger, materialism, or love of money (idolatry), gluttony, lust/porn/sexual sin, lying, theft, idolatry, jealousy, covetousness, slander, gossip, self-righteousness, pride (or the opposite: self-condemnation or self-hatred), etc. It also includes things like doubt, unbelief, rebellion, manipulating and controlling others, laziness, bitterness and unforgiveness, depression, despair, hopelessness, cowardice, fear of man, anxiety, etc. If we are honest, many of us would admit that we struggle with some of these issues to some degree, but if we are in Messiah, Romans 8:1 we are *not* under condemnation. But if we truly belong to Him, it is not only Yahweh's perfect will and <u>desire</u> that we be freed from such things - He has made a way for us to do it through the power of His Word and His indwelling Spirit! He loves us *as we are,* but as we continue to walk with Him and seek Him, His love and grace *transform* us and don't allow us to remain where we are.

The objective of this book is to dismantle the lie that we can be a "saved sinner," "sinful saint" or "born-again" believer who tolerates and practices sin in our lives. The truth is, according to Scriptures we already covered, Yeshua *cannot* be our Savior without also being our LORD who we follow, emulate, and obey in the power of His Spirit! As we read in 1 John 1:3-6 and Acts 5:32,

And by this we know that we have come to know Him – if we <u>keep</u> His commandments. The one who says, "I have come to know Him," but does not keep His commandments, is a liar and the truth is not in him; but whoever <u>keeps</u> His Word, in him the love of God has truly been perfected. By this we know that we are in Him: the one who says he abides in Him ought himself to walk in the <u>same manner</u> as He walked;

And we are witnesses to these things, and so also is the Holy Spirit whom God has given <u>to those who obey Him</u>.

We can all agree with this because the Scriptures clearly teach it, but what many *do not* agree with and even label heresy is that we as believers also are <u>not</u> destined to live in a *daily* or *perpetual* state of <u>struggling</u> with sin and *fighting* to <u>overcome</u> the sin nature – because as we have already seen in Scripture, by our union with Yeshua, we have His indwelling Spirit and resurrection power to overcome it <u>now</u>, not tomorrow, next year, or once we get to the "sweet by and by." Just like our born-again experience, victory over besetting or habitual sin and addiction can happen in a moment!! This does <u>not</u> mean we do not belong to the Lord and stand condemned if we have certain sins or addictions that we are fighting to overcome. However, if that is our *perpetual* state of being and we don't truly desire and endeavor, by the Spirit, to overcome sin (by realizing we are *already* holy and clean through our union with Yehusa), that is a sure sign that we must be born-again. If we are *entertaining* sin or *willfully* making room for it and giving ourselves over to it without any concern because we think, *"God is loving and gracious, so He's got my back; my sins are covered by the blood of Christ and I'm under grace, not law,"* then according to Scripture, we are surely lost and know *nothing* of the transforming power of God's love and grace. But if you feel the Spirit convicting you of your righteousness in Him if and when you sin, and you really *desire* to glorify Him and walk in the victory, freedom and joy He has for you - I want to tell you that through Yeshua and the power of His indwelling Spirit, *you do not have to tolerate sin or allow it to dominate your life another day*; you are <u>not</u> obligated, doomed, or destined to sin simply because you are made of flesh and bone! As we have seen, His Word says that if you are in Messiah, you are <u>not</u> merely human, but a "new creation" or species– the old has gone and new has come, and it is no longer *you* who live, but Yeshua who lives in you, and as He *is,* <u>so are you</u> *in this world,* Amen?! (2 Cor.5:17; Gal.2:20-21; 1 John 4:17).

We read in Hebrews 10:14, *For by one offering, He <u>has</u> perfected for <u>all</u> time those who <u>are</u> sanctified.* The Greek word for sanctify, *hagiazo,* does <u>not</u> mean to "purge and purify over a period of time," but to *set apart or make separate for God.* Time is not some magical ingredient that produces our holiness – any more than time plus chance produced evolution! Some translations of this verse render it as, "those who are *being* sanctified", but this is simply saying that God *has* perfected (past tense) those who *are* (present tense) coming to faith and being sanctified or set apart by their newfound faith in the Messiah. As we saw earlier, Yahweh says in Ezekiel 36: *"I will <u>give</u> you a <u>new</u> heart and put a <u>new</u> spirit in you; I will <u>remove</u> from you your heart of stone and give you a heart of flesh."* This "heart transplant" is <u>not</u> a lifelong process! When you became a new creation, the Lord ripped out that sin-loving, unbelieving, hateful, bitter, prideful, depressed, anxious, fearful, rebellious heart and He gave you HIS heart - a new, righteous, loving, tender, believing heart that loves God's Law and overflows with the fruit of His Spirit! Just like circumcision, something was completely *cut away* – in this case, *the old Adamic sinful nature.* Colossians 2:11 says:

Through our union with Him, we have experienced circumcision of the heart. All of the guilt and power of sin has been cut away and is now extinct because of what Christ, the anointed One, has accomplished for us. (TPT)

This means spiritual circumcision is not a *daily process;* it was a one-time occurrence when you became one spirit with Yeshua. Wouldn't you agree that Yahweh would be a cruel masochist if He made our entire life a long, bloody open-heart surgery or circumcision, removing our old heart piece by piece? When the same word for sanctify or sanctification is used in other verses, none of them require a time element. For instance, Yeshua told us to pray in Luke 11, *"Our Father, who is in heaven, hallowed* (or hagiazo) *be your name....."* Does this mean the Father's name is *becoming* sanctified or holy? Of course not. Or when Yeshua said in John 17, *"I sanctify* (hagiazo) *Myself for them, so that they also may be sanctified by the truth."* Is Yeshua saying He *gradually* set Himself apart for the Father (e.g., spending His whole life to get cleaned up or to become qualified)? Of course not - He was "set apart," period, just like all of us who have become one with Him! We read in Acts 20:32:

"And now I commend you to God, and to the word of His grace, which is able to build you up and to give you the inheritance among all those who ARE sanctified."

The Greek says, *"having BEEN sanctified."* What I am saying is that sanctification does NOT have to be a grueling, joyless, life-long process that all of us were told it is. If we are going to be accurate, sanctification is <u>not</u> a "process," but a <u>Person</u>, as we read in 1 Corinthians 1:30:

But by <u>His</u> doing, you are in Christ Jesus, <u>who became to us</u> wisdom from God, and righteousness, <u>sanctification</u>, and redemption.

Yeshua IS, not just *will be,* our wisdom and our righteousness. He IS, not only *will* be, our <u>sanctification</u> – and of course our redemption or salvation. You may ask, *"Are you saying we are perfect and therefore have no excuse for <u>not</u> living a fully sinless, sanctified, or holy life 24/7?"* Yes and no, because we understand that our salvation won't be *fully* or *completely* realized and experienced until the Lord returns, as the Bible also teaches that while we <u>are</u> saved, we are also <u>being</u> saved and *will* be saved (See Eph.2:5,8; 1 Cor.1:8,18, 15:2; 2 Cor.1:8, 2:15; Rom.5:10, 8:24,29-30; Mk.13:13). In this sense, salvation is not just an event, but also a process (as opposed to the Greek mindset, Hebraic thinking allows the tension between "both/and," rather than insisting something must be "either/or"). However, it is vital to understand that it is <u>not</u> the process of trying to *obtain* something we do not yet have or asking God to do what He has *already* done; it is the process of *maturing in our revelation of who we <u>already are</u> and what we <u>already have been given</u> through our union with Yeshua.* Once we begin to truly see (beyond doctrine alone) that we do not have to strive to *become* holy or beg to be *made* holy because we already <u>are</u> holy and sanctified by our union with Yeshua, what used to be a constant struggle increasingly becomes an effortless and joyful reality! This may sound like a matter of semantics or mind-games, but it isn't. If we do not truly believe that we *already are* saved (from sin) and that we truly *already are* holy or sanctified and set apart, we will find ourselves lowering our theology or interpretation of Scripture to the level of our *experience*, or lack thereof, and falling into the trap of attempting to merit and obtain *through the flesh* our union with God that has already been given to us as a gift by grace through faith alone in the <u>finished</u> work of His Son! It may be true that we were born with a sin nature we didn't *choose* (through Adam), but it is also true that we were born-AGAIN with a nature we couldn't *earn* (through Yeshua, the *last* Adam)! Author and revivalist John Crowder puts it this way:

The point of the gospel was to graft you fully into this union as an instant gift. And yet, we do not deny that there is a process of maturation and growth in this union. Consider the analogy of a vine and a branch. It is impossible for a branch to grow any closer to the vine than it already is. The two are physically connected. There is no breach that is progressively being filled. Now, does the branch continue to grow? Yes! It even flourishes, buds, and bears fruit. But is it growing <u>toward</u> union, or <u>because</u> of union?..... It is not that our hearts and emotions are being more and more deeply united to Christ. They are tied into the wine vine right now. But love is bursting and flowering out of us now in greater and greater degrees....

A sapling is of the same substance as the mighty oak. One may be more mature than the other, but both are fully and completely still <u>trees</u>. We are all now the same substance and body of Christ. We are all the same substance of holiness, whether sapling or fully grown. I'm not really moving deeper into union or getting closer to God. I'm already fully connected to the Head. Our union has been procured. Rather, I am drinking deeper from that very real and complete union that I already have. [Consider the analogy of marriage]: the more I enjoy my wife, I am not becoming more married to her. I'm enjoying the marital connection that we <u>already</u> have. Think of your marriage contract as faith that binds you. But marriage without love is just a piece of paper....

Love always grows. The love I have for my wife grows every day, but my union with my wife is not incomplete today merely because I will love her more tomorrow. I even believe that the love of God is a growing, expanding thing.....His glory always increases. The more his personality is revealed to me, I effortlessly reflect and manifest his nature like a mirror - His nature that I <u>already</u> possess. (Crowder, *Mystical Union;* Sons of Thunder Publishing, pp.199-201)

Sadly, religion or "churchianity" will label this as heresy, not because Scripture does not affirm or teach it, but because it sounds too simple and too good to be true – that Christ really did kill our old man and transform our nature down to the very core! But I'm learning that if I hear a Gospel message that sounds too good to be true, it likely is - I just have to shed the religious traditions of man that have invalidated and diluted the Word to fit their experience or lack thereof! I'm discovering that when the Gospel is preached in its simplicity and purest sense, the religious community will quickly reject it as heresy or blasphemy, which is exactly why they continue to struggle with sin – which may manifest as legalistic self-righteousness or self-condemnation (as well as sickness and disease, as many reject the belief that the blood of Christ also purchased our *physical* healing and not just our spiritual healing, even though the Scriptures clearly affirm this). But back to my point: if we find ourselves in what seems to be a never-ending battle with sin issues in our life, or worse, we aren't grieved about routine sin in our lives, we need to do some serious "soul searching." Keep in mind that "routine sin" is <u>not</u> confined to sins of immorality, As we read in 2 Corinthians 13:5 and 2 Peter 1:10, we must "examine" ourselves to see if we are "in the faith," and "make our calling and election sure."

This question may arise: *"If we shouldn't have to 'fight' or contend with sin and a sin nature, why are we told to 'put on the full armor of God' in Ephesians 6, and why did Paul say he 'beat' his body to make it his slave, and as he told Timothy, 'Fight the good fight of faith'?"* We are not in denial; there indeed is a fight. But let me repeat, just like the "process" is not about becoming someone we <u>already</u> *are* in the spirit, the "fight" is <u>not</u> about struggling to obtain a victory that is *already* ours by our union with Yeshua. This begs the question: so why do we need armor and weapons, which clearly imply there is a fight, battle, or struggle? Again, because there is a fight – the fight (by the SPIRIT) of *exercising our faith to live out who we <u>already</u> <u>are</u> AS SONS OF GOD* (See 1 Cor.9:25-27; II Tim.2:4-5; Gal.3:3,5:22-23; Rom.8:13). *It is the fight of remaining focused and keeping our minds in alignment with the truth and reality that we have <u>already</u> won the war over Satan, sin, and temptation (along with sickness/disease, poverty, depression, fear, trauma, etc.)!*

This is what Yeshua was getting at when He said in Matthew 6:22: *"The light of the body is the eye. If your eye is single, your whole body will be flooded with light."* In other words, if we keep the eyes of our hearts *only* fixed on the truth of who we are in the Lord, His light and glory will flood our entire being, causing our outward lives to manifest that very light (see Isaiah 60)! And our spiritual armor and weaponry serve to deflect and extinguish every flaming arrow of deception from the enemy, reminding him (and ourselves) that because of what Yeshua accomplished on our behalf, we are not fighting FOR victory, but FROM a position of victory - which makes all the difference in the world! As His Word says, we are (present tense) *more* than conquerors through Christ, or as some translations render it, "overwhelming victory is ours," He *always* leads us in "triumphal procession" because we are called to reign in *this* life, not just the life to come! (Rom.5:17,8:37; 2 Cor.2:14). This means we are not striving in the flesh to <u>obtain</u> something we do not yet have; through the Holy Spirit and the Word, we fight to daily appropriate, walk in, and maintain what is *already* ours by grace through faith. This "fight" really isn't a fight as we normally think, where we toil, struggle, or strain. Because of the finished work of

Yeshua, who overcame sin and evil on our behalf, our warfare is "fought" from the posture of supernatural *rest, peace,* and *joy!* That is the overwhelmingly "Good News" of the Gospel! As John Crowder also writes:

Cease resisting the old [man]. *You must rest in the new. Take no thought of how to overcome evil. Disregard altogether a sin consciousness. Let your eye be single, full of light. In everything, see Christ alone. Do not look for devils behind every bush. View temptation even as a positive adventure, for by rejecting the false, you are affirming the opposite.* (Crowder, *Mystical Union*, Sons of Thunder, 2010, p.88).

If we continue to reduce the victory the Scriptures say we have to mere doctrine, or relegate it to a future time, we will keep striving and shadow boxing to win a war that has already been won on our behalf. What good is a theoretical or "doctrinal" victory that cannot be experienced in the *here and now*? And what is a "doctrinal victory" anyway? If our victory in Christ is confined to the *spiritual* realm, where it has no physical, practical, and tangible impact in our daily lives, it doesn't do us any good *here and now*. If our understanding of the victory we have in Christ is only a *future* and not *present tense reality*, then yes, our fight <u>will</u> be from a place of strain or struggle. We may even find ourselves fighting from a place of anxiety or fear, because we are in a *defensive* posture trying to protect and maintain (by the flesh) what we have by grace through faith, not realizing that in Christ we are on the *offense* – called, commissioned, and empowered to take on new territory and have the <u>enemy</u> in a place of terror because he sees we have awakened to the truth of who we really are in God and who He is in us! Satan trembles at the thought of us awakening to the truth that *as* (Yeshua) *is, SO ARE WE <u>in this world,</u>* because he knows such revelation will lead to his demise! Yes, because of what our Lord did and our union with Him, Satan has *already* been defeated and we are fighting <u>from</u> victory, not *for* it, but only as we grow in revelation of our identity in Yeshua will this victory increasingly manifest itself!

CHAPTER 9

The Power of Thinking & Speaking Like God
"But we have the mind of Christ" **1 Cor.2:16**

Many believers would say it's *impossible* to "think like God" for the obvious reason that *we are not God!* As Yahweh Himself said in Isaiah 55:8-9: *For My thoughts are <u>not</u> your thoughts, and My ways are <u>not</u> your ways, for as the heavens are higher than the earth, so are My ways higher than your ways, and My thoughts than your thoughts."* Paul also says in 1 Corinthians 2:9: *<u>No</u> eye has seen, <u>no</u> ear has heard, <u>nor</u> the heart* [mind] *of man imagined, what God has prepared for those who love Him.*

First, as we saw earlier in Ephesians 5:1, we are commanded to *imitate* God, which clearly implies that by His Spirit indwelling us, we *can* and *should* imitate Him. Of course, this does not mean we are to "try" to act or behave like God in our own strength or self-resolve. That is not only impossible, but will only produce dead works and burn out! But imitating God, in and by His Spirit, does not only apply to us walking in love, as Paul says in verse 2, but we are to imitate and manifest the nature of our heavenly Father in *every* way. The perfect picture of what it looks like to emulate the Father is Yeshua, who is the radiance of His glory and the exact representation of His nature, and in whose steps we are commanded to follow (Heb.1:3; 1 John 2:6). But let me reiterate: seeking to follow in the steps of Yeshua or to imitate the Father <u>in the strength of our *flesh* or *willpower*</u> is not only impossible, but such efforts will bring us under the condemnation and judgment of His Law. As noted earlier, if we live by the Law, we will die by the Law; if we trust in our law-keeping to place us in right standing with God, we will be fatally judged by it.

Secondly, when most believers quote Paul in 1 Corinthians 2:9, they stop right there, not realizing that he was quoting Isaiah 64:4, which was written *before* Yeshua renewed the Covenant by His shed blood or sacrifice. If we keep reading, Paul shows us that *now*, by Yeshua's shed blood which renewed the covenant, we CAN **_know the things freely given to us_** by Yahweh (v.12)! He says we can know what saints of old did *not* know because unlike them, we have the Spirit of God *indwelling* us, **who <u>reveals</u> to us the deep or hidden things of God!** He also spoke of making *"the Word of God <u>fully known</u> – the mystery hidden for ages and generations, but has <u>now been revealed</u> to His saints"* (Col.1:25-26). As Yeshua said, *"Many prophets and righteous people longed to see what you see, and did <u>not</u> see it, and to hear what you hear, but did <u>not</u> hear it"* (Matt.13:17). Now, through Christ and His blood, we are habitations of His very presence and seated with Him in heavenly realms; we *share* in God's divine nature and are *one spirit* with Yeshua; we have His mind and "know all things";[27] we are "imitators of God," created to "be like" Him and even privileged to release the supernatural miracle-working power of His Spirit! (See 2 Pet.1:4; 1 Cor.2:16,6:17-19; 1st John 2:20; Eph.2:6,5:1,4:24; John 14:12; Mark 16:17-18).

It is true that our union with the Lord will *never* be severed, but do we literally know "all things" or know God's thoughts and reflect His nature at every moment? Of course not – not only because our revelation of Him is progressive, but because our level of engagement with the Lord and our pursuit of our inheritance and destiny in Him fluctuates as fickle human beings! We are all commanded to "work out our salvation," but while some of us pursue our inheritance and destiny in the Lord with spiritual tenacity and "violence," others will bear little fruit either due to just plain laziness and apathy or because of all the distractions and worries of this life (Mk.4:19). The point is, because we are joined to the Lord and are currently spiritually seated with Him in heaven, we have direct and constant *access* to His manifest presence, limitless power, and thoughts! Paul affirms this when he speaks of the *riches of the glory of His [God's] inheritance in the saints, and the <u>exceeding greatness</u> of His power <u>toward us</u> who believe, according to the working of His mighty power which He worked in Christ when He raised Him from the dead,* and said that God is able to do <u>exceedingly abundantly</u> *ABOVE all that we ask, think, or imagine, <u>according to the power that works in us</u>* (Eph.1:18-19, 3:20) Let this truth sink in!

This means that if we want to truly practice thinking like God, which is ultra "positive thinking," and reap its practical benefits, we must align our thoughts, beliefs, and perspectives with *HIM* and *His Word!* There is nothing more positive, uplifting, and encouraging than God's Word, which should be our primary source for renewing our minds and spirits. Learning from books on self-development is fine, as long as any counsel we receive and apply to our lives ultimately aligns with God's truth and we are depending on the *Holy Spirit* for true change or transformation, not ourselves or others. But we need to understand that "self-help gurus" or "shrinks" did not invent the idea of "positive thinking." Positive or right thinking originates with our Creator and Father, which is why we look to HIM first and foremost. In Luke 8:18 and 11:34, He does not merely suggest or encourage, but <u>commands</u> us to be careful of what we *hear* or *listen* to, and that if our eye (the "lamp" of our body) is healthy, our whole body will be filled with light. Through Paul, He <u>commands</u> us to *think positively* by meditating on things which are true, honorable, right, pure, lovely, etc., to set our *minds* on things *above*, <u>not</u> on earthly things, and to fix our (spiritual) eyes on the *unseen* and *eternal* realm rather than things which are seen and temporal (Phil.4:8; Col.3:1; 2 Cor.4:18). And as Yeshua said, if we want to physically see or experience His glory and kingdom, we must *first* believe or stand in faith even when we do <u>not</u> see. When Mary was grieving over the death her brother Lazarus, the Lord told her in

John 11:40, *"Did I not tell you that if you <u>believed</u>, you would <u>see</u> the glory of God?"*. The world, along with many "unbelieving believers," won't believe *until* they <u>see</u>, agreeing with the motto, "seeing is believing". But in the Lord's kingdom, *believing is seeing* (or at least opens the door to seeing)! This is why Paul prayed that the "eyes" of our hearts would be *enlightened,* that we may <u>know</u> the hope of our calling and the riches of the glory of God's inheritance in His people (Mark 4:24; Luke 11:34; Phil.4:8; Col.3; 2 Cor.4:18; Eph.1:18).

Paul wrote these verses because Holy Spirit revealed to him that right *living* is the natural by-product of right *believing* and "seeing." He couldn't have said this more clearly than in Romans 12:2:

Do not be conformed to this world, but be <u>transformed by</u> the <u>renewing</u> of your <u>MIND</u>, that you may prove what the will of God is, that which is good, acceptable, and perfect.

This means that if we try to change or modify the exterior (our behavior/habits) before the interior (our spirit/soul) is changed and transformed, we live with the inner dissonance, turmoil, and dilemma that Paul spoke of in Romans 7, which we addressed earlier. ***If we are "trying" to be a "good Christian" and "trying" to please God by avoiding sin and keeping His laws, we need to do a religious "de-tox" and renew our minds with the truth of God's Word, which tells us that the fruit of godliness is the natural by-product of abiding in Yeshua, the true Vine*** (John 15:5). Does an apple tree strain to produce apples? If the conditions are right, it *effortlessly* produces apples because its roots are firmly planted in good soil. Similarly, if we are truly born-again and are abiding in the Lord, we cannot *help* but produce the fruit of joyful obedience and godliness! As He also said in John 15, if we abide and remain in Him as a good tree that *cannot* bear bad fruit, we will bear *much* (good) fruit! But if our walk of faith has always seemed difficult for us and God's commands have felt like a heavy or burdensome chore, we need to do some self-examination, considering the possibility that we need to be truly born-again, so that God's grace and love will inspire and empower us to *effortlessly* keep His laws and manifest His nature or likeness, rather than us trying to produce the fruit of His Spirit through the arm of the flesh (e.g., relating with God through His Law rather than by His love and grace). Here are some more verses which prove that God's grace, if it is received rightly, produces an obedient and righteous lifestyle:

For the <u>grace</u> of God has appeared, bringing salvation to all men, <u>instructing us to deny ungodliness and worldly desires and to live sensibly, righteously and godly in the present age</u>... (Titus 2:11-14)

...Jesus Christ, through whom we have received <u>grace</u> and apostleship <u>to bring about the</u> <u>obedience of faith</u> among all the Gentiles for His name's sake,....(Rom.1:5; See also Rom.16:26)

... that the name of our Lord Jesus will be <u>glorified</u> in you, and you in him, <u>according to the grace of our God</u> and the Lord Jesus Christ. (1 Thess.1:12)

....it (the gospel) is constantly bearing fruit and increasing, even as it has been doing in you also since the day you heard of it and <u>understood the grace of God in truth</u>. (Col.1:6). (In other words, if we fail to understand God's grace in accordance with truth, we receive His grace in vain and it does not produce the effect He intended).

The Word also says, *<u>examine</u> ourselves to see if we are in the faith; make every effort to confirm our calling and election; for this is the love of God, that we keep His commandments; and His commandments are <u>not</u> burdensome* (2 Cor.13:5; 2 Pet.1:10; 1 John 5:3). As we saw earlier, this is also why Yeshua told the Pharisees to *first* clean the <u>inside</u> of the cup, so that the <u>outside</u> may *also* become clean. I know I am being redundant and belaboring the point, but it is vital that we grasp this truth.

As believers, we all understand that obedience and righteous living is important to Yahweh. Actually, living godly lives or according to His Word is so important that without it, we will never see Him or enter His kingdom (Heb.12:14; Matt.5:8). But again, it is time for us to realize that the Lord is <u>not</u> looking for mere behavior modification or for those who do their best to observe His "list" of laws or commands. The kind of godliness or purity He is looking for is not superficial or outward, nor is it rooted in things such as self-resolve, willpower, a sense of duty or obligation, or even good intentions and motives. Is it not possible to have a "clean" or pure motive to please God while not truly knowing Him? Our righteousness must spring from the core of our being or our spirit, where the Spirit of Yeshua dwells. If we *know* that we are the righteousness of God in Christ and not ourselves, as 2 Corinthians 5:21 tells us, our everyday lives will naturally and increasingly manifest that righteousness (e.g., when it has moved from *information* or mere doctrine to *revelation,* or we know it in our spirit-man and not just our mind). This means the only way our lives can truly be transformed to reflect Yahweh's image and likeness is by changing how we *think* and what we *believe.*

Some of what I will share in this lengthy chapter may sound like the "self-help power of positive thinking," but the truth is, if there is power in negative thinking (as we noted earlier), that means there is also power in "positive" thinking. Droves of "awakened" <u>un</u>believers are discovering this, but just because an unregenerate person uses spiritual principles, truths, or axioms to their advantage certainly does not negate them or make them evil; nor does it make it wrong or unbiblical for a *believer* to utilize them (the opposite is also true: just because a person may not know the Lord does not mean spiritual/unseen laws cannot work for them; if the physical laws which God established apply to every human being, and not just His children, it is no different concerning spiritual laws). Excuse the cliché, but we should have enough discernment to avoid "throwing the baby out with the bathwater"! Because the Lord fashioned all humans in His image and likeness, a person does not need to be born-again to experience the benefits that come from applying the various truths or principles and spiritual or unseen axioms He has established at creation. Why wouldn't an <u>un</u>believer not be able or allowed to benefit from observing Yahweh's laws? Obeying His laws may not spiritually save them, place them in right standing with Him, or open the door to the Lord's personal favor, but it certainly can save them much physical and/or emotional *pain* and *misery* caused by sin or lawless living! If we are to ever come into maturity as sons of God, we must be those who *"by practice, have had our senses trained to discern between good and evil,"* and by the Spirit, have learned to *"test all things and <u>hold on to the good</u>"*- or as we say, to "eat the meat and spit out the bones." (1 Thess.5:21; Heb.5:14).

At this point, many authors of books like this would make a disclaimer, such as: *This book is <u>not</u> intended to address issues concerning harmful addictions, habits, or serious emotional and psychological issues; Please see a licensed professional for such things.* Statements like that could help protect the author from certain legal ramifications, but the truth is, there are situations when it may be necessary to see a licensed professional or doctor - <u>not</u> because God's Word and faith alone is insufficient to experience freedom and victory, but simply because our faith has not yet developed to the level required for us to go that route. As we are maturing in faith and becoming more grounded in the Word of God, there will many be times when we need help from others– which is perfectly fine because that's how the Lord works to bring His Body into maturity (see Eph.4:11-14). But if we are aggressively pursuing spiritual maturity, because God wants to bring us from co-dependence to interdependence, there will be times when He will lead us to fight certain battles *without* the aid of others, where it's just us and Him, so that we will become more established in faith and *experientially* learn the power of His Word (as we can know the power of His Word in our *minds* without knowing it in our <u>hearts</u>). These are also times when we experience significant growth in our revelation of our true identity, inheritance, and authority in Yeshua, and begin to walk it out in a more tangible and practical way.

This might sound far off from you or that it's unattainable, but let me tell you: if you are struggling to overcome sinful habits or strongholds and self-destructive thought patterns: THERE IS HOPE! With the Lord's empowering love and grace, there is *always* hope! As Hebrews 10:23(TPT) says: *we must cling tightly to the hope that lives within us, knowing that God always keeps His promises!* But just like our faith, this hope we have in the Lord and His promises is not passive, in that we have no role to play. We cannot sit on our backsides, physically or spiritually speaking, waiting for God to just "zap" us with healing, deliverance, or "greater" faith. Yes, ultimately it is the Lord who brings us into healing and freedom, as He is the Author and Finisher of our faith, but the Lord tells us through Paul that <u>through His Spirit's power</u>, *we* are responsible to "put off" the old man, to be renewed in the spirit of our mind, and to "put on" the new. He said in Ephesians 4:22-23, Romans 8:13, 13:14, and Galatians 5:16:

For if, <u>by the Spirit</u>, YOU put to death the misdeeds of the body, you will live;

[YOU] clothe yourselves with the Lord Jesus Christ, and [YOU] do not think about how to gratify the desires of the flesh;

[YOU] walk by the Spirit, and YOU will not carry out the desires of the flesh.

Verses like this are <u>not</u> talking about making salvation and victory over sin a work of our flesh or will-power and self-resolve. Albeit unwittingly, all of us have been guilty of attempting to do just that, and we eventually got burned-out or discouraged. The point is, while we will never truly overcome sin or the flesh *by* our flesh, our flesh is physically involved (just as confession of the Word *alone* does not bring supernatural results in our life, it is nonetheless required for walking in our victory). It is vital that we "work out our salvation" *in and by the Holy Spirit*, <u>not </u>our own strength or efforts. Take a moment to read Jeremiah 17:5-8, where Yahweh gives a clear warning to those who trust in themselves and how trusting in Him will bring great blessing and cause us to bear much fruit in our lives, even in troubling times.

This may sound obvious, but it is important to understand that habits that we feed will *grow*, and habits that we starve will *die*. This not only applies to sin, but also to false and damaging doctrines we have learned. What we *think* about and how we see ourselves (or how we have been *taught* to see ourselves) is a huge part of it. It is *vital* that we do <u>not</u> identify ourselves with or by our sin, behavior, or addiction. Many of you may know this, but unless it has changed, Alcoholics Anonymous has their members introduce themselves to the attendees by saying *"Hello, my name is _____; I am an alcoholic."* They confess this <u>even if</u> they haven't touched a drink for a long time, because their motto is: "once an alcoholic, *always* an alcoholic." But if a person's goal is to beat their addiction to alcohol, this is a terribly self-defeating confession to make! Repetitively thinking and saying to yourself: *"I <u>am</u> and will <u>always</u> be an alcoholic"* will make it much more difficult, to say the least! Imagine a person who is addicted to cigarettes or pornography and who desires to overcome them, saying, *"Once a porn addict, <u>always</u> a porn addict!"* This could apply to <u>any</u> addiction – for example: TV, sugar/chocolate, food in general (ouch!), exercise, work/busy-ness, or emotional issues like anger, depression, fear, bitterness, etc.

Our beliefs and our mouths can cause us so much pain and trouble! As Proverbs 6:2 and 12:13 say, our words can *ensnare* or *trap* us. In other words, *we are hung by our tongue.* There is a huge difference between *acknowledging* your sin or being honest about it and finding your *identity* in it. If we are battling with sin as a believer, we should not deny it or lie to ourselves about it, but if we *define* ourselves by that sin or habit, our focus is on the <u>problem</u> rather than the answer or *solution*, and as a result, we unknowingly *feed* or *empower* the very thing we so desperately want to overcome. You see, just as the Lord established physical laws to govern the material universe, He also established <u>spiritual</u> laws to govern the *unseen* realm. One of those laws, as previously mentioned, is the law or principle of sowing and reaping. For instance, if we sow seeds of life, blessing, encouragement, healing, or prosperity (even when we do not presently *see* them), we will eventually *physically* reap and manifest fruit which affirms, validates, or aligns with those good seeds. As those who are fashioned in the likeness of God and are commanded to imitate or emulate Him, we have delegated power and authority to call things that are not *as though they are* (Eph.5:1; Rom.4:17).[28] Of course, droves of Christians (and charlatans or imposter) have grossly abused this power for selfish purposes, but again, such abuse obviously doesn't negate or invalidate spiritual truths and our position of authority in the Lord, nor mean that we can't use and steward them *rightly* or as God intended.

Unfortunately, this power can also work in a very negative and damaging way, and our Enemy not only knows this very well, but takes advantage of it as much as he can. Because Satan was not created in the image and likeness of God, he does not have the ability to create; he can only counterfeit, distort, and pervert the truth through deception and lies. This is why he has to find a vessel who will agree with his lies (albeit unwittingly) and give them substance through speech or words. Because we are fashioned in our Lord's likeness, our tongues have the ability or power to create circumstances that bring either life and blessing, or death and cursing. For example, if we sow seeds of fear, death, doubt, sickness and lack or poverty, it is only a matter of time when those seeds will *physically* produce fruit which validates and aligns with those bad seeds. Again, *as a man thinks in his heart, so is he* (Prov.23:7). And as we read in Galatians 6:7-8,

Make no mistake about it, God will never be mocked – for what you plant will always be the very thing you harvest. The harvest you reap reveals the seed that was planted. If you plant corrupt seeds of self-life into this natural realm, you can expect to experience a harvest of corruption. If you plant the good seeds of Spirit-life, you will reap the beautiful fruits that grow from the everlasting life of the Spirit. (TPT)

Yeshua affirms this in Mark 11 when He said: *"Whoever says to this mountain, 'be taken up and cast into the sea,' and does not doubt in his heart, but believes what he says is going to happen, it shall be granted him."*[29] 1 John 5:15 says, *if we know that He hears us in whatever we ask, we know that we have* [present tense] *the requests which we have asked from Him.* I will repeat: this not only applies to biblical and positive beliefs or declarations, but includes unbiblical and negative or even demonic declarations, such as: *"I'm such a messed-up sinner," "Because I'm only human, I will always have to struggle with sin and temptation," "Every time flu season comes around, I'm bound to get it!" "I NEVER have enough money to pay all my bills.....money leaves my hands as quick as I can earn it!" "I have clinical depression," "Until I get to heaven, I'll have to accept and tolerate sin, sickness, and disease as a normal part of life – we all have to die one day anyway!" "This medical condition (sickness/disease or addiction/habit) has run in my family DNA for generations – I've inherited it, so I have to deal with it too!",* Etc. Such declarations will *affirm, establish,* or *solidify* "mountains," obstacles, and problems in our lives, not destroy or remove them!

Am I saying we should *deny* our problems exist or lie about our condition or circumstances? For example, if a doctor were to give us a diagnosis of some terrible disease like cancer, God hasn't called us to deny reality by saying something like, *"No that's not true, your test results are inaccurate or lying - I don't have cancer."* As imitators of God, we <u>don't</u> speak that which exists as though it *doesn't exist* (e.g., your body having cancer), rather we are to speak what does <u>not</u> currently exist in the physical realm as though it *does* (e.g., your body <u>is</u> healed of all cancer or is free of all infirmity). We don't deny reality or call our doctor a liar, rather, we make sure not to honor and empower the diagnosis or condition by *agreeing with* it and *owning* it. Not affirming a diagnosis may sound like we're denying its reality, but not agreeing with it (for example, its finality) does <u>not</u> mean we are ignoring or denying what is happening in the physical realm - in this case, what is going on inside our body. What we *do* deny is its right to dominate, control, overpower or influence us in ways that are contrary to God's promises and provisions that are ours in Yeshua! The world around us and the bad or evil things we see and experience are real, not illusions. However, there is an *unseen* reality that is greater, higher, or *superior* to what we <u>do</u> see. Doesn't 1 John 4:4 say that *He who lives IN us is greater than he who is the world?* If we are going to call anyone a liar in such cases, we would call the DEVIL a liar, and we refuse to give him power by agreeing with any such evil report because God's Word explicitly and emphatically tells us that we are and WERE healed by the Lord's stripes! (Is.53:5; I Pet.2:24-25; Matt.8:17).

This applies to *every* area of our lives, including relationships. To one degree or another, all of us have suffered some form of emotional or physical abuse or trauma in our life, and without being aware of it, we end up filtering life and our relationships through the lens of such traumatic experiences – even if we have forgiven those who have offended us or sinned against us. Our painful experiences can either affect how we see our heavenly Father and how we relate with Him, and/or how we see others and relate with them. We may not speak it or even be conscious of it, but we establish mental strongholds and make inner vows such as: *"I will never be like my father/mother"*, *"Sooner or later, everyone I get close to will end up betraying me in some way" "Nobody can be trusted!" "I'll never open my heart again to let someone hurt me or take me for granted!" "I don't want or need friends because they all eventually turn their backs on me, take advantage of me or let me down!" "All men/women are [fill in the blank]," "God is always angry [distant, disappointed, disgusted, etc.] with me because I always mess up or never measure up to His expectations,"* Etc.

Such beliefs and declarations stem from a victim mentality and cause us to isolate or distance ourselves from others and close our hearts, as well as cause *them* to want to distance themselves from *us*. But if we keep reminding ourselves that our old self *already died,* that we are one spirit with Yeshua, and are our lives are hidden in Him, we can be fully released from the pain and trauma of past hurts; we no longer have to live in a spirit of offense or feel we must defend, protect, or emotionally isolate or distance ourselves. Do dead people get offended or erect walls to defend themselves? No! Do dead people get revenge or hold feelings of anger, resentment, bitterness, and unforgiveness towards others? No! Do dead people close their hearts and avoid being open and transparent with others because they fear being hurt, rejected, betrayed, or let down again? No! Are dead people contentious, easily angered, or do they keep record of wrongs against them? No!

We may object: *"But God gave us feelings or emotions, and we are human beings, not robots or machines! And we certainly can't let others treat us like a doormat or take advantage of us!"* Of course, we should love ourselves by not allowing others to walk on us because as humans, we all have feelings or emotions. But it is a mistake to assume that all of our emotions are acceptable or healthy and godly.

Most of the emotions we learned to have in reaction to hurtful or painful events in our lives did <u>not</u> come from the Lord and are anything *but* healthy or godly; just like sin, such emotions were inherited from Adam. Feelings and reactions such as bitterness, unforgiveness, resentment, distrust, defensiveness, pride, control, unrighteous anger, anxiety, paranoia, and fear of hurt or betrayal may indeed be "normal" or even "expected" for us as humans, but if we are joined to the Lord and share His nature, they are *anything <u>but</u>* normal and should be repented of and forsaken! If the believers in Corinth were admonished for behaving like "mere men" because they were "new creatures" in Yeshua, what makes us think *we* can use the excuse, *"But I'm only human!"*? This toxic cocktail of emotions is not only opposed to the nature of Yeshua that we now share, but it also grieves and quenches His Spirit, causes much damage to our relationships <u>and</u> bodies, eventually creating sickness and disease (or dis-ease)!

Additionally, they open doors to the Enemy or give him a foothold in our lives! Why would we want to hold on to the *old* self when the Lord invites us to "put on the new self" in Him and be made "new" in the attitude of our minds – and thereby walk in true freedom! Amen?! (See Eph.4:20-24). And we all know I Corinthians 13, the "love chapter" often read at weddings. It says love is patient, kind, forgiving, humble, is not easily angered or provoked, does not make a list of wrongs suffered, etc. Then Yeshua tells us that we are *blessed* and that we should *rejoice* when people hate us, speak evil of us or spitefully use us (Luke 6:22; Matt.5:44). But most believers do the opposite – instead of rejoicing, they complain, close their hearts, hold grudges, get even, or "punish" those who hurt, offend, or disappoint them through gas-lighting[30] or the silent treatment of passive aggression! Such reactions to sins committed against us only place us in a worse position and invite curses or open doors for the enemy in our lives.

For many of us, it seems our default is to agree with and speak negativity and that which condemns, curses, and even sabotages our lives. Why is it so natural or easy for us to align with the enemy (albeit unwittingly), but it seems so hard to speak and agree with God's Word and promises over our lives - not just with our minds and lips, but with our hearts or emotions, as though His Word was *already* fulfilled? Why is it so easy to hear the enemy's voice, but recognizing the voice of our Shepherd Yeshua seems to be difficult? The most obvious reason could be due to disobedience; if the Spirit of God has spoken but we have repeatedly ignored and disobeyed His voice, whether it involves big or small issues, it is foolish to expect Him to continue speaking or to give us more revelation. As He said in Luke 12:48:

"From everyone who has been given much, much more will be demanded, and to whom they entrusted much, of him they will ask all the more."

Another reason we may not hear His voice clearly, as I have already pointed out, is due to the false teaching or doctrines that have been handed down to us. While it is surely possible, it is difficult to unlearn, break away from, and rise above that which has been engrained in us for many years or even decades. It is difficult to hear the truth if our minds are clogged and our vision is obscured by false ideas and paradigms. As the old adage goes, "you cannot teach an old dog new tricks." It all comes to down to our hearts or convictions and what we truly believe, because as Yeshua said in Luke 6:45 and Matt.12:36-37:

"Out of the abundance of the heart, the mouth speaks".

"I tell you, on the day of judgment people will give account for every <u>careless</u> word they speak, for by your words you will be <u>justified</u>, and by your words you will be <u>condemned</u>".

Wow – our Lord says our words can either *justify* us or *condemn* us! This makes our tongues a "double-edged sword" for blessings or curses, which means we should be very intentional about the words we are "broadcasting" into the spiritual realm *and* physical – whether we are speaking of ourselves or others. Another well-known verse is found in Matthew 7:1-2:

"Judge not, that you be not judged. For with what judgment you judge, you will be judged; and with the measure you use, it will be measured back to you."

Unbelievers or the world refers to this principle as karma or the law of attraction,[31] but these words clearly refer to the biblical and spiritual law of *sowing and reaping*, which most of us confine to judging *others*. But these words also apply to judging ourselves. Without realizing it, how often do we judge ourselves in ways that *condemn* us or keep us in *bondage, captivity,* or a position of *victimhood* (such as the examples mentioned earlier)? If you have been led to believe that you are an unworthy "worm," "wretch," or "sinner," that your heart is sick, wicked, and depraved, or that you will never be free from sin and temptation until you die, what do you think such beliefs will manifest in your life? As we read in Proverbs 18:6-7:

A fool's lips bring strife and his mouth calls for blows. A fool's mouth is his ruin, and his lips are the snare of his soul.

One of the most powerful gifts we have been given is our free will or the power of choice. But if we do not use it wisely or responsibly, we can find ourselves stuck in perpetual cycles of self-sabotage. Many Christians have bought the lie that as long as they love the Lord and are living righteously, His perfect will or destiny for them will assuredly and naturally come to pass, quoting Jeremiah 29:11, a verse we all love to claim. Unless we repent, we can be sure that entertaining and tolerating sin will keep us from stepping into the purposes God has for us, but it is also possible that we can truly love Him, know His Word well, and walk in obedience to His commands, and *still* never fulfill our destiny in Him. As I said earlier, one of God's promises is that He is "obligated" to fulfill *His promises* in our lives, but He never promised, nor obligated Himself, to fulfill *our potential*. He indeed "knows" the plans He has for us, but we have a vital role to play in seeing those plans materialize or brought to fruition – and not only through obedience to His commands, which should be a given. We may very well be observing God's laws out of love for Him, but oftentimes we can overlook or minimize issues and faulty convictions or beliefs of the heart and mind.

Did you know that your beliefs and convictions about yourself can dominate or even negate what the *Lord* believes about you or how *He* sees you? Of course, it is not that what He says about us becomes false by our words, but if His declarations have no effect on us because our unbelief and negativity block our hearts from receiving them, they might as well be false! Many believers would object, saying, *"What?! My thoughts or words about myself can <u>never</u> minimize God's words over me or make them ineffectual! God is GOD, and what He says WILL happen no matter what – as He said in Isaiah 14:24, 'As I have planned, so shall it be, and as I have purposed, so shall it stand'!* Yes, we can find many such verses that speak of God's ability to accomplish His will and purposes, but as we have noted, we must allow the Scriptures to interpret themselves and avoid building doctrines off just one verse here or there. There are many passages of Scripture that would show we cannot take verses like Isaiah 14:24 to mean His plans for us will come to pass with or without our faith and obedience, for He also said in Isaiah 1:19-20, *"IF you are willing and obedient, you will eat the best of the land, but IF you resist and rebel, you will be devoured by the sword."*

In other words, while Yahweh's love for us is unconditional, His promises concerning His <u>plans</u> for our life are *conditional*, not automatic or guaranteed, as Psalms 95 and Hebrews 3 tells us how God's people did <u>not</u> enter into His rest or the "Promised" Land because they constantly provoked Him with their unbelieving and straying hearts. If our belief, words, and actions have no impact on God's will and purposes for our lives, why did an angel shut Zacharias' mouth due to his doubt concerning the prophecy that he and his wife would give birth (to John the Baptist) at such an old age? The angel said to him in Luke 1:20, *"Behold, <u>you shall be silent</u> and <u>unable to speak until</u> the day when these things take place, for you did not believe my words, which shall be fulfilled <u>in their proper time</u>."* If those words are only figurative and not literal, why did the angel make Zacharias mute for several months? If God's will and purpose for our life automatically comes to pass in our lives, regardless, why did Paul tell Timothy to "make war" or "fight the good fight" *in accordance with the prophecies previously spoken over him?* When the Bible says the power of life and death are in our tongues, and the Lord said "may it be done unto us *as we have believed*" did He not truly mean it? Yeshua said many times in the Gospels, "AS you have believed" or "ACCORDING to your faith, <u>so let it be done unto you</u>". He also said our words can justify or condemn us and that we are judged for every *careless* and *lifeless* word we speak. Should we not take Him seriously?! If we truly belong to the Lord, that "judgment" doesn't mean we will be shut out of the kingdom, but it certainly can mean our destiny in this life can be missed or even aborted (until we repent and start becoming more thoughtful and disciplined with our beliefs and confessions over ourselves).

Verses such as those we just read in Isaiah did <u>not</u> change once Yeshua renewed the covenant by His blood. He said in Mark 7:13 that the Pharisees were guilty of making the Word of God "of no effect" or even "void"! How? By holding on to their man-made traditions that caused them to violate and undermine the Scriptures. If we can invalidate God's Word or render it ineffectual in our lives by our traditions (which often seem harmless), then we can certainly do the same through our unbelief, doubt, and negativity! You can desperately beg, plead, fast, or cry out to God for Him to help you overcome a sin or addiction, or for Him to give you a miraculous healing or financial breakthrough, but if you cannot first envision or SEE yourself free from sin or SEE yourself free from sickness and disease or lack and poverty, you will remain stuck, sick, and locked into a position of lack and bondage – even though the Lord has *already* provided the victory through His blood! Many of us have tried affirmations or declarations to no avail, and wonder, *"If God's Word says my tongue has the power of life and death, and that I will be satisfied with the fruit of my lips, where is that fruit?!"* First of all, we must be sure our prayers or declarations are in alignment with God's Word and nature, otherwise we pray amiss and will not receive. If we are praying biblically, yet still don't see the results, it may be due to one of these following reasons: Either we must be patient and keep sowing seeds of faith and trust, knowing that if we do not grow weary and lose heart, we WILL reap a harvest in God's perfect timing, or it is because there is no coherence between what we outwardly *declare* with what we inwardly *believe*. You can verbally declare over yourself all day, "I am liberated from that sin or addiction!"; "I am whole and healed!" or, "I am prosperous and walk in abundance!" but you will get nowhere if your <u>emotions</u> (which flow from the core beliefs of your heart) are saying: "<u>But</u> I am an addict!"; "<u>But</u> no matter how hard I try, I *cannot* overcome this sin!"; "<u>But</u> my body says I *am sick!*"; "<u>But</u> I *cannot* afford to pay my rent and I am broke!" "<u>But</u> I *feel*.....But I *believe* I am.....(a sinner, sick, poor, depressed, rejected, etc.)."

It is the "but" which reveals where our problem lies. When Isaiah 55:11 says the Word shall *not* "return empty" without accomplishing God's desire or purpose in our lives, it assumes that our FAITH is pure (without mixture or double mindedness) and fully engaged, as we saw earlier in Hebrews 4:2 that the Word will <u>not</u> profit us if it is not coupled or mixed with faith. Our faith is our agreement or our "Amen!" to God's Word, as His Word says there is power not only in vision, but also in *agreement,* which implies unity or coherence. When we use our sanctified imaginations to mentally "see" new ways of being and acting, coupled with true faith and the emotion that comes with having *already* received that for which we are asking, the breakthrough, miracle, or victory *will manifest itself* in due time - assuming that what we are desiring and declaring aligns with God's Word and nature!

This is how we meditate on what GOD says about us and what He has already provided for us, and in doing so, we are literally or physically *re*-minding and rewiring our minds, which leads to transformation and healing (as we saw in Romans 12:1-2). If you *wait* for the answer, miracle, or victory to come *before* you give the Lord thanks and praise, you may be waiting a very long time, because faith does not say "I believe I *will* have it one day" or, "I know God is *able* to do it" (even Satan knows God is "able"!); rather, faith says, "Even though I do not see it with my natural eyes, I believe I have it NOW and I give thanks that God has *already* provided!" Faith simply rests in a position of joy, peace, and gratitude, knowing the *physical* manifestation of what has already been done in the spirit is coming at the right time. When and how the Lord releases it should not be our concern; we just know that we <u>know</u> He will fulfill His Word, and we give thanks for it! When we truly accept and receive it in our spirit, we will, in time, receive it in our body or life. As we read a moment ago, Yeshua said in Mark 11:24, *"I say to you, all things for which you pray and ask, <u>believe that you have received them</u>*

[past tense]*, and they shall be* [future tense] *granted you.*" If we pray in alignment with the Lord's Word and nature, we can be sure that our requests are already answered, for He will not say "no" to that which He has already said "yes."[32] As Paul wrote in 2 Corinthians 1:20, *for all the promises of God in Him* [Yeshua] *are "Yes" and "Amen," to the glory of God through us.* Likewise, He will never change His word or mind about us in order to accommodate our doubt or negativity.

Again, if we are to receive, we must persevere in faith and patience. As Paul said in Galatians 6:9, we cannot grow weary or lose heart, for *in due season we <u>shall</u> reap!* If we ever receive a breakthrough or miracle *in spite of* our unbelief or lack of faith, it is <u>not</u> because God changed His word or mind because He will never do so, but simply because He is gracious and merciful, as His kindness leads us to repentance (keeping in mind that repentance starts with a change in MIND, not behavior)! But because He wants us to mature in our faith and revelation of who we are in Him and what we've already been given by our union with Yeshua, He most often will allow our begging and orphan-mindset to receive its reward, which is *nothing.* Believers are not peasants or orphans who beg; we are sons who should be *full of expectation and faith* that our Father will in time fulfill or perform His Word in our lives

(Jer.1:12; Is.66:9)! We must remember that without faith it is impossible to please God (Heb.11:6)! Does not James 1:6-7 clearly tell us that if we are double-minded, we will not receive *anything* from the Lord? And how often did Yeshua rebuke the disciples for their unbelief, doubt, or lack of faith? Again, Yeshua said several times, *"As YOU have believed, so <u>let it be done to you</u>."* Again, this not only refers to beliefs that bring *blessing* and *favor* into our lives, but whether we like it or not, it includes those which bring *curses* and *pain or sorrow* into our lives. As we read in Proverbs 13:3, 14:3, 18:20-21,

By the mouth of a fool comes a rod for his back, but the lips of the wise will preserve them; those who guard their lips preserve their lives, but those who speak rashly will come to ruin; From the fruit of a man's mouth his stomach will be satisfied; he is satisfied by the product of his lips. Death and life are in the power of the tongue, and those who love it will eat its fruit.

Again, most Christians have been taught to avoid this topic because it is "New Age" and "name-it-claim-it" or "blab-it-grab-it" teaching. Certainly, many self-promoting charlatans in the Church have taken things to extremes or have abused universal laws and truths which God has established, but we must ask: *Does a law or truth become invalid, obsolete, or dangerous simply because many abuse or misuse it?* No, for as we noted earlier, just because one person abuses God's laws does not mean others *cannot* use them or benefit from them as He intended. If we do not deny or avoid observing laws established by our government simply because they are often abused and violated, why would we do so with any of the laws our *Creator* established (whether they involve things in the seen or unseen realm)? Again, we must "test all things and hold on to the good," learning to "eat the meat and spit out the bones."

I believe another reason why many believers avoid this topic or take issue with it is due to FEAR; it can be unnerving or scary to think we have that much power, authority and responsibility with our words – and as they say, we fear, mock, and reject what we do not understand. It may also be pride that keeps us from being corrected because we cannot accept the idea that we have been wrong about something for so long. But as those fashioned in His image and likeness, Yahweh has indeed given us power and authority, as Yeshua says in Luke 10:19, *"Behold, I have given you <u>authority</u> to tread on serpents and scorpions, and overcome <u>all</u> the power of the enemy, and nothing by any means shall harm you."* And as most of us know, when He commissioned His disciples in Matthew 28, immediately after

He says, *"All authority in heaven and earth has been given to Me,"* He tells them, *"Go, <u>therefore</u>, and make disciples of all nations."* In other words, He was "passing the baton" to His followers, His future disciples (you and me), as He clearly said in John 20:21; 14:12:

"As the Father has sent Me, so I send YOU; He [anyone] *who believes in Me will do the <u>same</u> works that I do – even <u>greater</u> works than these shall he do, because I go to My Father."*

We must stop diluting or watering down the words of our Messiah out of false humility or in efforts to justify our sin of doubt or unbelief and a life that is void of the miracle working power of God! If He said we will do the same works He did, and even greater, it is *faith,* not arrogance, to really believe Him and go for it! If we are commanded to walk as He walked and do the works He did, it must be possible - in His power, of course! Aren't "all things possible for him who believes", and can we not "do all things" through Yeshua who gives us strength?! (Mark 9:23; Phil.4:13)

It ultimately boils down to this: will we really believe the prison door is not only unlocked but *wide open?* Will we dare to believe that we've *already* been set free – not only from the eternal consequences of our sin, but from sin itself? Again, if we cannot truly be liberated from sin until we physically die, that would make *death* our savior, not Yeshua! The truth is, Romans 6 and Colossians 3 tell us that we (our old or sinful self) *already* died and that "he who has died is freed from sin" (as dead men do not sin)! It is time for us to believe that through Him, ALL things are truly possible, and we can do ALL things in Him who gives us strength! Let us be bold and childlike in our faith to believe that our old carnal man or Adamic nature *truly* died with Yeshua (not just figuratively). Let us truly believe that we have been raised to new life in Him and are now <u>one</u> spirit with Him, where it is no longer *us* living but Christ living in and through us! Let us take God at His Word that truly, no weapon formed against us shall prosper (unless we let it) and that as He IS, <u>so are we</u> in this world! Many of us know these Scriptures well, but as I pointed out earlier, many of us are still reading the Bible as a religious textbook and do not truly understand that it really is *living and active*, and that it does <u>not</u> return empty if we agree with it and declare or confess it over our lives! We need to stop reducing it to ink on paper and truly believe it and begin walking it out, because what we sow and believe <u>inwardly</u>, we will in fact, in some way or another, <u>outwardly</u> reap in our everyday lives. In other words, our thoughts and beliefs or convictions determine our choices and actions– which in turn impact our relationships and everyday *circumstances*. What this means is that if we allow the enemy to sow <u>his</u> seeds into our minds (which is anything that opposes faith and conflicts with God's Word and will), whether we like it or not, we *will* reap the consequences – both spiritually *and* physically.

But how do we renew our minds like Romans 12 says? We renew our minds by coming into agreement with God or by aligning our thoughts and beliefs with the <u>truth</u> of His Word –casting down every thought or imagination that is contrary to the knowledge of Christ (2 Cor.10)! This means that if you give the enemy power by agreeing with the lie that you are "just a weak and depraved sinner" who "must accept" that sin and temptation will often get the upper hand in your life, then do not be surprised with the bad fruit such stinking thinking produces – *which is a perpetual battle and struggle with sin in your life!* As the saying goes: Garbage in, garbage out! As noted, *we cannot consider ourselves DEAD to sin like Romans 6 commands us while maintaining the confession that we are a "sinner" who will always battle or struggle with it!* If you are desperate to see transformation in your behavior and thought life, and are tired of the enemy getting the upper hand in your life through sin and self-condemnation, the first step is <u>not</u> to change the fruit, which is your *conduct* or *behavior*, but to change the <u>root</u>, which is how you think and how you <u>see</u> yourself by *renewing* your mind and aligning it with the truth of God's Word! If you have the root of God's Word in your heart and mind, like a tree, it will naturally and effortlessly produce the fruit of joyful obedience and righteousness!

CHAPTER 10

As He is, So Are YOU!

I have been crucified with Christ, therefore it is no longer I who live, but Christ who lives in me;.....as He is, so are we in this world. **Gal.2:20; 1 John 4:17b**

I have already given you many "keys" to walking in victory over sin and temptation, but here is the most important one, which I touched on in the beginning of the book. Lacking knowledge or revelation of who we truly are in the Lord is why so many of us as believers live *way below* our inheritance as sons of God, and why so many of us constantly struggle with sin issues and tolerate things like guilt and shame, depression, pride, sickness, poverty, anxiety, despair, etc. Of course, we are not under condemnation because such things still exist in our lives, but this explains why there is so much pain, conflict, discord, confusion, and division in our lives, relationships, and bodies. There are other contributing factors of course, but ultimately it can be boiled down to this *one* underlying issue we already touched on: we are suffering from a serious IDENTITY CRISIS. Some may say relationship or intimacy with God is the key, and that would also be true, as relationship and identity should be inseparably connected. I use the word "should" because many believers know Yeshua enough to be born-again, but their everyday lives and struggles reveal that they know very little concerning their identity in Him. Others may have a great *head knowledge* of their spiritual identity or know the Scriptures very well, but that knowledge has yet to become *revelation,* where it increasingly transforms their lives in every area. Simply put, as believers, we do not truly <u>know</u> who we are in the Lord, who He is in us, and what He accomplished on our behalf. Isaiah 51:1 says:

"Listen to Me, you who pursue righteousness, who seek the Lord; look to the ROCK from which you were cut, and to the quarry from which you were dug."

In other words, if you're seeking or striving to be righteous, you must remember that you are a "chip off the old block" - the block being Yeshua, our Rock! He is your Elder Brother, and you are His offspring, through which He "prolongs His days" in the earth! (Heb.2:11,17; Is.52:10). Because you are indwelt by His Holy Spirit, are one with Him, and share His nature, that means YOU are also holy! You are His "portable" Tabernacle or habitation, and because He promised to never leave you, that means wherever He is, you are, and wherever you go, He goes with you! He clearly said, in John 12:26 and Matthew 28:20: *"Whoever serves Me must follow Me, and <u>where I am, there my servant will also be</u>; <u>I am with you always</u>, to the end of the age."*

This may sound strange, but putting it in modern terms, this makes us His "avatar." Doesn't the Bible say that we are His *temple*, that we are Christ's "members" who collectively make up His "Body," and that it is no longer we who live, but Christ who lives in us? (1 Cor.6:15,12:27; Eph.3:6, 5:30; Gal.2:20). Most of us confine the term "body" to the definition of a physical group, congregation, or mass of people. While it certainly includes that, we need to realize that when the Bible speaks of the "Body of Christ," it also carries a spiritual or mystical connotation. As members of His Body, we are His *embodiment* or the physical expression and demonstration of His Person, power, and presence on the earth! We are not called to simply represent Him; we are called and privileged to *re-present* Him! When God took on flesh or human form in His Son, He made it possible for Him to *continue* doing so throughout history through His people. That may sound weird, but it is biblical. Colossians 2:9-10 and 1 John 4:17b say:

For __in Him__, all the fullness of Deity __dwells in bodily form__, and in Him __you__ have been made complete.....";.....for as He is, __so are we in this world__.

It is important to note that John 4:17 says we are like our Lord as He IS *now,* __not__ as He was during His earthly ministry. What this means is that we identity with the *resurrected, ascended* and *glorified* Christ who overcame the world and all the works of the Enemy! Many believers are trying to emulate Yeshua *before* He fulfilled the Law, *before* He established the new covenant, and *before* He won the victory and sat down at the right hand of the Father! It is very important to understand that when we try in our own strength and resolve to "act like" Jesus or "copy" His behavior, we've adopted a "do-it-yourself" mentality, living as though we are *separate* from Him – which is precisely where the spirit religion or religiosity will take you. Most Christians would object: *"But John also says in 1 John 2:6 that we must 'walk as He walked' or 'follow in His footsteps,' so how could it be religious or mean I'm trusting in my own strength by endeavoring to imitate His life?"* The key to understanding this verse rightly is found in the first half, which many believers leave out. It says: __Those who claim to ABIDE (or live) in Him__ must walk as He walked. John is saying that if you claim to abide in Christ, or if you claim to be united to Him and to know Him in a personal way, your life __must__ prove or affirm that union. However, it's not that you keep God's commands and try to live an outwardly righteous life to prove you are in union with Christ or that you are intimate with Him – because even some unbelievers and atheists live a more clean or moral life than many believers do! But if you truly abide in Yeshua, keeping the commands will *always* be the natural byproduct because through His indwelling Spirit, His "spiritual DNA" is now a part of YOUR spiritual makeup! As Paul said in Galatians 2:20, *it is no longer I who live, but Christ who lives IN me!*

When our focus becomes behavior or outward conformity to God's Law, we've unwittingly unplugged ourselves from the Power Source by seeking to establish our own righteousness through law-keeping. You must know that God is not calling you to "fulfill" the Law or to defeat sin – that was *Yeshua's* job and only HE could do it (and He DID it, as He said on the cross, "it is <u>finished</u>!"). Your only role is to BELIEVE and REST in His finished work and to ABIDE in Him or stay connected through intimacy and fellowship. When you make that your priority, living out the Law and walking in HIS victory over sin will become more and more natural and even effortless! You don't even think about "keeping the Law" because you are aware of the truth that you now share the very nature of your heavenly Father and Savior, and that He has already sanctified you or set you part for Him. If you understand and believe you are holy by nature by your union with Him, everything falls into place naturally! This is what Jesus was getting at when He said His yoke is easy and His burden is light!

Let me go back to Colossians 2, where it says "all the fullness of Deity dwells in bodily form." We know this is talking about the Lord, but it's also talking about His people. We read about this in Isaiah 53:10, when it says the Lord Yeshua, through His death, shall "see His *seed* [offspring or descendants]" and "*prolong* [extend] His days". [33] We know that Yeshua never married or had physical children, so this "seed" clearly refers to *us*, His people, disciples, or followers! He clearly said in John 12:24, *"unless a grain of wheat falls to the ground and dies, it remains by itself. But if it dies, it produces much fruit."* Yeshua is the "grain of wheat," and <u>we</u> are the *fruit* His death and resurrection produced! Meditating and "chewing" on such truths will bring huge transformation in our lives! If we are going to fulfill the Lord's declaration in Matthew 5:14 that *we* are the light of the world because THE Light of the world dwells within us, we must begin seeing or envisioning ourselves in this light (pun intended)!

We read in Lamentations 1:9 that because God's people did not realize or consider their destiny, their "collapse was awesome" or "their fall was astonishing." And as we have seen in Hosea 4, Yahweh says, *"My people are <u>destroyed</u> for <u>lack of knowledge</u>."* We simply do not know who we are! Hosea goes on to say that it was not only their *lack* of knowledge that brought their downfall, but it was because His people *rejected* knowledge – which required a *willful* and *conscious* act. Being uninformed due to laziness or false teaching is one thing, but *willfully* rejecting knowledge or what we <u>know</u> to be true is entirely different! Considering we have the written Word, the Bible, AND the *Living* Word, Yeshua our Shepherd, who teaches and leads us by His indwelling Spirit, we will surely be held accountable for spiritual laziness or for remaining uninformed and ignorant. We will be held accountable for not "testing all things" and for not "studying to show ourselves approved." But will He show mercy toward us for knowingly *rejecting* His truth and turning a deaf ear to Him? (See Is.65:12; Jer.17:3).

"Rejecting" His truth is not only manifested through rebellion and living in sin. We also can be guilty of rejecting His truth when we refuse to be corrected and admit that we are wrong concerning our understanding of His Word in particular areas. On some level, every one of us hold to certain doctrines or theological paradigms that we have embraced all our lives that can keep us from receiving the revelation Yahweh wants to release to us. **While it is true that He will never violate or change His perfect and everlasting Word, He has no problem with violating our *faulty interpretations* and *applications* of it.** For Him to do this, we must not only be humble and teachable, but we must *ask* the Lord to change out our old wineskins (false man-made doctrines) and give us the capacity to receive the "new" wine of His Spirit, which is the fresh revelation and enlightenment of His established Word that we have yet to see or understand (See Luke 5:33-39). We can also be guilty of rejecting His

Word or what He says about us through unbelief and false-humility, which come in the form of self-condemnation – we simply can't see ourselves the way *God* sees us because we're too focused on our weaknesses, failures, and sins of the past. But Philemon 1:6 says our faith becomes effective by *acknowledging* <u>every good thing which IS (not will be) in us in Christ Jesus</u>. This means our faith is weakened and ineffective when our eyes are fixed on *ourselves* rather than Yeshua who lives in us. As we covered earlier from 2 Corinthians 3:17-18, we are increasingly transformed into the image of our Lord as we behold Him or gaze upon Him with the eyes of our hearts. **"Gazing" at yourself or being fixated on your sin, shortcomings or inadequacies, along with your attempts to imitate the life of Christ in your own strength, only feeds the power of the flesh and keeps you in a perpetual cycle of self-sabotage.**

Let me shift gears and say some things that might shock you, but give me a moment to explain and prove how biblical it is: If you are a *born-again believer indwelt by the Spirit of Yeshua:* There is <u>nothing</u> you can do to make God love/accept you more than He already does. There is <u>nothing</u> you can do *to make yourself* holy or righteous before Yahweh. There is <u>nothing</u> you can do to *qualify* yourself or to *merit* the anointing of God's Spirit to share the gospel or to even heal the sick, cast out demons, and raise the dead. There is <u>nothing</u> you can do for God to give you *more* faith or *more* of His Spirit than what He gave you at the moment of your conversion or born-again experience.

Does this mean we don't *grow* or *mature* in our <u>intimacy</u> with the Lord and our <u>experiential knowledge</u> of Him, or that we shouldn't we *pray, fast,* or *study* and *memorize Scripture* more? Of course we grow and of course we should do those things, but as we covered earlier, we do <u>not</u> mature in the sense that we *become* "more righteous" in God's eyes, obtain "more faith" or *become* "more qualified" for God to use us; surely we become more righteous in a practical, physical, and visible way, but that righteousness naturally springs forth as we mature in our <u>understanding</u> and <u>revelation</u> of the righteousness we *already HAVE* and who we *already ARE* by our union with Him! But didn't the disciples ask Yeshua to "increase" their faith in Luke 17:5? Yes, but He didn't lay hands on them and say, "Ok – now you've got it!" Rather, He made it clear that it was not about the *quantity* of their faith, but the *quality, purity* or *focus* of it. It wasn't that they needed "more" or "greater" faith, but about using the faith they <u>already</u> had - as He said that if their faith was *like* or *as* a mustard seed, they could uproot a mountain![34] We have been taught that God has given some people great faith and others just a little, quoting Romans 12:3, *"God has allotted to each a measure of faith.* But in the original manuscripts, it is "THE" measure, not "a" measure, meaning God didn't give different amounts of faith to each of us and then unfairly expect all of us to walk in the same manner His Son did! The faith you have isn't your own anyway; it is a <u>gift</u>, and you could not have truly confessed 'Jesus is Lord' *except* by the Holy Spirit (any more than Peter did when he acknowledged the Lord's true identity in Matthew 16:17). The SPIRIT of GOD is the one who enabled you to "see" Yeshua as Lord and Savior or who enlightened the eyes of your heart, and even granted you the gift of godly sorrow or repentance (See Eph.1:17-18, 2:8; 1 Cor.12:3; 2 Cor.7:10; Phil.1:29; John 6:65; 2 Tim.2:25). Paul says in 2 Corinthians 3:17 that the Holy Spirit is the Lord *Himself,* and because He cannot give what He does not have, He gives us HIS faith. In the original text of Mark 11:22, Yeshua did <u>not</u> say, *"have faith <u>in</u> God,"* but have the faith OF God. In essence, He was saying, "Have God-like faith".

But again, this is impossible; we can't create or generate faith on our own – otherwise, Yeshua lied when He said, *"Apart from Me you can do <u>nothing</u>,"* and, *"the flesh profits <u>nothing</u>; it is the <u>Spirit</u> who gives life"* (John 15:5, 16:3) We also read in Zechariah 4:6, *"not by might nor by power but by MY Spirit" says the Lord.* If we cannot produce faith to be born-again or truly see Yeshua as Lord apart from His Spirit giving us revelation, why do we think we can generate faith in our own strength to love His Word or ways, overcome sin, and to live righteous or holy lives? And why did Yeshua tell us to have a faith we <u>cannot</u> create or generate on our own? He wasn't trying to frustrate us, but to help us reach the end of ourselves, causing us to cry out to HIM, our *only* Source of power and salvation. The gift of faith which redeems, saves, or justifies us (and will glorify us) is the *same* gift by which we naturally live an obedient and sanctified or holy life. We do not start the race by *faith* and then hope and try to cross the finish-line through the efforts of our *flesh, self-resolve* or *willpower* (see Galatians 3).

The point I'm making is that it does not require more faith to be born-again and *cleansed* from sin than it does to live in victory *over* sin and to live obedient, godly lives; it does not require more faith for God to heal a headache that it does for Him to heal us of cancer or even raise the dead! How could it require more effort on God's part to forgive and purify us than it does for Him to *heal us emotionally and physically*? As Yeshua said in Matthew 9:5, *"Which is easier to say, your sins are forgiven or rise up and walk?"* If we are born-again and the Lord's Spirit indwells us, He *already* loves and fully accepts us; by our union with Yeshua, we are *already* clean, holy, and blameless before God; because Yahweh stands outside of time and space, He sees the finished product, which means in His eyes, we *already* look like Yeshua and have <u>all</u> the power needed to live in victory over sin. And because His Word says the same Spirit that raised Him from the dead lives in us, in His Name and in His power, we can do the <u>same</u> and even *greater* miracles than He did when He physically walked the earth!

By the way, if you have a hard time having faith that Yeshua wants to flow through YOU to perform miracles such as healing the sick, casting out demons or even raising the dead, keep in mind that faith for walking in the miraculous is NO different than faith for walking in righteousness or living in victory over sin and temptation! How is that? Because walking in obedience and godliness (joyfully and naturally by the Spirit) is just as "miraculous" or supernatural and spiritual as being used by God to perform healing miracles. If we disagree and think *we* decided to love God and His laws, and *we* decided to walk in His ways by our own strength and will, or that God uses us in miraculous ways because of *our* goodness and faith, we are in the very dangerous place of trusting in our flesh and establishing our own righteousness! Yes, if you are in Christ, He did not repent *for* you or *make* you surrender your life to Him; *you* chose to do so, but as we just covered, that would have been <u>impossible</u> apart from His Spirit opening your eyes and granting you a godly sorrow that leads to repentance (2 Cor.7:10; 2 Tim.2:25).

We already discussed this, but the repetition is meant to help you absorb the material. If we find ourselves exasperated because we are constantly struggling to overcome sin and to live obedient, righteous lives, it is simply because we are trying to do it in our own strength, self-resolve, or willpower. What believer would think that *they* (in and of their own power), can perform a healing miracle or expel a demon or unclean spirit? Hopefully no one! The Lord indeed gave His followers the command: "Heal the sick," implying that we, in and of ourselves, have the ability to do so. But believers who heal the sick or perform any other supernatural feat should know full well that it is not *their* power or *their* holiness which brings the miracle, but as Peter made clear in Acts 3:11-16, it is <u>faith</u> in the *Lord's Name* and HIS power and presence flowing *through* them which brings the miracle. We also read in Mark 16:20 and Hebrew 2:4:

And they went out and preached everywhere, <u>while the LORD worked WITH them</u>, confirming the Word by the signs that followed; And <u>GOD</u> confirmed the message by giving signs, wonders, various miracles, and gifts of the Holy Spirit according this <u>HIS</u> will.

God's people are just willing and obedient conduits of His power and presence, and again, it is *no* different when it comes to living in victory over sin (and sickness/disease) and temptation or walking in righteousness. As we yield to Yeshua within us, His SPIRIT produces the fruit in and through us (Gal.5:22). As we saw earlier in Galatians 2:20-21:

I have been crucified with Christ; it is <u>no longer I who live</u>, but <u>Christ</u> who lives in me. The life I live in the body, I live by faith in the Son of God who loved me and gave His life for me.

We also looked at chapter 5, verse 16, which tells us that if we *walk by the Spirit, we <u>will not</u> carry out the desire of the flesh.* As noted earlier, refusing to fulfill the desires of your flesh does <u>not</u> enable or qualify you to walk by the Spirit, rather, walking by the Spirit is what empowers you to say no to sin and temptation. If we vainly attempt to subdue and kill our flesh *by* our flesh or willpower, we will remain in a never-ending battle with sin and find ourselves feeding and empowering it! As Yeshua said in John 3:6; 6:3:

"The flesh gives birth to <u>flesh</u>, but the Spirit gives birth to spirit; the flesh profits <u>nothing</u>; it is the Spirit who gives life,"

And Paul writes in Galatians 5:17:

.....for the flesh lusts against the Spirit, and the Spirit against the flesh, and these are contrary to one another, so that you do not do the things that you wish.

In other words, the spiritual fruit of holiness and power over sin and temptation will never come through physical, fleshly, or natural means. The key is knowing that because we share in the Lord's divine nature and are one spirit with Him, our old man or sinful nature doesn't need to be crucified because it *already was* by our union with Him! The deeper our revelation of this truth goes, the easier and more natural it will be to walk in the victory HE obtained for us.

Do you recall our discussion about the internal battle that exists within an <u>un</u>believer in Romans 7? Our efforts in the flesh that spring from self-resolve will *never* bring about the fruit of obedience and godliness that is supernatural yet natural in that it is joyful and therefore effortless! As Paul said in Galatians 3:3, *Are you so foolish? Having begun by the Spirit, are you now being perfected by the flesh?* He goes on to say that a righteous person lives righteously by FAITH and are blessed as "sons of Abraham" by FAITH, <u>not</u> by works of the law or their fleshly self-resolve and willpower to abstain from sin and keep God's laws. As noted, Paul is obviously *not* saying we are no longer required to keep God's Law simply because we are saved by faith, as he says the Law is holy and good IF we use it "lawfully" or as the Lord intended (1 Tim.1:8; Rom.7:12,22). We do that by keeping things in their proper order: law-keeping or obedience alone does not justify us or make us right with God, rather, our justification, which comes by grace through faith alone, *produces* obedience which springs from an inner transformation; as we saw earlier, we cannot kill the flesh *by* the flesh (self-resolve) or overcome sin and carnality by *natural* means or weapons, but only by the *Spirit* and His transforming grace.

The point is <u>not</u> that it is *impossible* to overcome addictions or bad habits by our own strength, willpower, or self-resolve and discipline (countless unbelievers do), but who do you think receives the honor and credit for that? Certainly not God! While living a righteous life is obviously important, it is *not* the ultimate goal in life. If it was, the Lord wouldn't care *how* we did it – just as long as we keep His laws and conform to His standards! But the God we worship and serve is not after mere "behavior modification" or outward conformity to His Word. His greatest desire is that we have an *intimate relationship with Him rooted in love* and that we bring HIM all the glory and honor. When this becomes our greatest priority and desire also, it will *naturally* and *effortlessly* produce the fruit of a righteous life, coupled with a disdain for sin and disobedience!

If we are a professing Christian who really knows what the Bible says about our identity and we can quote all the right verses, but we are still entertaining sin in our life, tolerating it, or struggling with it, then our problem isn't ignorance. Hopefully it isn't because we are in a place of anger, offense, and rebellion towards God. If that is the case, we need to do some soul-searching and repentance. If it is due to a spirit of apathy or complacency, we need to repent for that too, because the Lord did not die to purchase for Himself a spiritually lazy and distracted Bride, as Yeshua said in Revelation 3, *"Wake up and strengthen what remains and is about to die.....because you are lukewarm, and neither hot nor cold, I will spit you out of My mouth."* Lastly, it may be because we do not *truly* believe what God's Word says about our identity, which would make us an *"unbelieving believer."* (If that title intrigues you, you can watch my YouTube videos entitled "How to NOT be an Unbelieving Believer"). If we want to experience the victory God says we have over the enemy, sin, and temptation, while there isn't a "formula," it *does* require these 4 "ingredients," if you will:

1) Because the enemy thrives on our ignorance, we must KNOW the Word of God, remembering, as we covered earlier, that it is <u>not</u> God's invitation for us to simply have sound doctrine and head knowledge. While sound doctrine is obviously vital because the Word is the foundation of our faith, we can have all our "theological

ducks in a row," have a seminary degree, or be a pastor yet still live a powerless life or not even know the Lord personally. That would be tragic because the Scriptures are an invitation to *encounter* God, to truly *know* Him and to be *transformed* by His Spirit to the degree that we reflect His image or re-present His likeness. As we addressed earlier, while we certainly should be students of the Word and pursue the <u>Word</u> of God, we should never do so *at the expense* of pursuing GOD of the Word! See Acts 4:13; John 5:39.

2) We must have FAITH that Yahweh's Word is actually <u>TRUE</u> *here and now*, and that it applies to each of us *personally* in very practical and life-altering ways. We know that without faith, we end up reducing the Word to a book of principles and spiritual concepts that have little to no impact in our lives concerning the transformation, freedom, and healing the Lord purchased for us. The Word of God does no good if it is not united with and empowered by *faith,* without which, it is *impossible* to please God. See Heb.4:2,11:6.

3) If we <u>know</u> the Word well and have true, biblical faith, as we covered throughout this book, our faith must effortlessly manifest itself by our walking in joyful OBEDIENCE <u>and</u> POWER. 1 Corinthians 4:20 says *the kingdom of God is not a matter of talk, but of <u>power</u>,* and 2 Timothy 3:5 says we can have a "form of godliness" while "denying its power" (in this context, "power" refers to the Gospel shaping us into the image of Yeshua, but the rest of Scripture makes it clear that it also includes us being conduits of God's miraculous power for healing and deliverance).[35] We've seen that the Bible makes it clear that if we are not being transformed into Yeshua's image by the Father's love and grace, which always leads us to obey the Word and live godly, we neither *truly* believe it nor love God.

4) If we are steadily growing in our knowledge and revelation of God's Word and our faith is proving itself through an obedient and godly lifestyle, we need to continually *confess* that Word so that God's glory, will and kingdom increasingly manifest itself on earth as it is in heaven. Hebrews 3:1 does not say Yeshua is the High Priest of our faith or our beliefs; it says He is the High Priest of our <u>confession</u>. Why? Because *nothing* is accomplished in God's kingdom without a *declaration* or *confession* of His living and active Word! This means confession leads to expression or manifestation, and our confession comes from our heart. We read in 2 Corinthians 4:13 that we *believe,* therefore we *speak,* and Romans 10:10 says that with the heart we *believe* and with the mouth we *confess,* which results in salvation. As already noted, millions of professing Christians abuse this truth by treating God like He is *their* servant, as though He were a "cosmic bellhop," using His Word like a slot machine or a mantra they can chant to manifest their selfish idolatrous desires and build their own kingdoms. They love to claim the first half of 1 John3:22, which says *whatever we ask we receive from Him,* but the second half of the verse places conditions on our receiving: <u>because</u> we <u>keep</u> His *commandments and do what pleases Him!* So many have bought the lie that because of Yeshua's sacrifice and God's grace, we can claim His blessing and favor, along with salvation, *regardless* of how we live. Hopefully most of us know that is a fat lie and understand that God's grace never excuses sin or frees us from God's Law itself – it frees us <u>from</u> sin and liberates us from "the law of sin and death" or the curses that came upon us for *breaking* God's Law – AND His grace *motivates* and *empowers* us to *effortlessly* and *joyfully* keep His commandments! (Titus 2:11-14; 1 John 5:3)

Considering the truths we have covered thus far, why do we ask: *isn't it <u>impossible</u> for a Christian to <u>not</u> sin?* Is it because we are trying to preserve our freedom to sin, to make room for sin in our lives, and to justify it? Why not instead ask: *is it <u>possible</u> for a Christian to <u>not</u>

sin? Didn't our Lord say "all things are possible to him who believes"? Didn't Paul write that we can "do all things through CHRIST who gives us strength," that our old self was *crucified* with the Lord so that our body of sin was *done away with,* and that we *have been freed from sin*? (Mark 9:23; Phil.4:13; Rom.6:6-7)? Why would it be heretical or crazy to agree with Scripture? Watering down the truth of Scripture to fit our experience (or lack thereof) is <u>not</u> the answer!

The Lie and Illusion of Separation

Let's briefly revisit the subject of identity. As we have seen, how we see ourselves (and God) is vitally important. If we think we are enemies of God, "wretched sinners" who are separated from Him, or believe He is angry, disappointed, or frustrated with us, that faulty internal perception will inevitably and naturally manifest and validate itself through our outward behavior. Romans 5:10 says *while we were enemies, we were reconciled to Him through the death of His Son.* Be sure you understand that WE were enemies, not God, and WE were reconciled to *Him;* He was not reconciled to *us.* If God was our true enemy because of our sins, He would not have sent His Son to reconcile us. It is not speculation for us to say we were only enemies of God in our *minds,* because Colossians 1:21 clearly says this:

And you were at one time strangers [separate from God] *and enemies <u>IN YOUR MINDS</u> as expressed* [manifested] *<u>through</u> your <u>evil deeds</u>.*

Paul affirms this in Romans 8:7a, which says *the <u>mind</u> set on the flesh is <u>hostile</u> toward God.* What this means is that all sin blinds us from the revelation and understanding of our identity as God's sons. [36] When we sin, our natural reaction is to feel guilt, shame, and condemnation, and we feel God is angry or even disgusted with us. We might envision Him standing over us with a scowling face with

His arms crossed and His foot tapping or a wagging finger in our face. Of course, this condemnation comes <u>not</u> from the Holy Spirit, but from the Enemy, the "Accuser of the Brethren." When we believe his lies that our heavenly Father has "had all He can take" or that He has turned His back on us, we end up distancing ourselves from Him or even want to "hide" – just like Adam and Eve did when they first sinned. Satan may even quote Scripture to us (as he did to Yeshua in the wilderness), such as Isaiah 59:2, *but your iniquities have made a <u>separation</u> between you and your God, and your sins have <u>hidden</u> <u>His face</u> from you so that <u>He does not hear</u>*. If we don't understand the glory of the renewed covenant we have in Yeshua and what His sacrifice accomplished, we'll read verses like that and say things like, *"Exactly! God has cut me off and He isn't going to hear my prayers because of my sin – so why pray or why read His Word? I probably lost my salvation at this point!"*, and as a result, believe we have to work our way back into good standing with God through our good works or performance. We assume Isaiah is saying God withdraws from us because of our sin, or that the wall between us and God was put there by HIM. But it doesn't say that – it just says sin creates a separation between us without telling us *why* or *how*. We also assumed this verse is saying our sins made GOD turn away from us, but no, it just says our SIN "hides" God's face from us. Why? Because sin causes us to be consumed with *ourselves* and make us think God can't "handle" engaging an unclean vessel. Lastly, we also assume Isaiah 59:2 is saying the reason God won't listen to us is because He's ticked off and disgusted with us because of our sin, and therefore can't or won't hear our prayers. The reason we read verses in that light is because we filter them through a sin-conscious lens.

In addition, most Christians believe the Bible says God is "too holy to look upon sin." It indeed says that, but this phrase is taken from only the first part of Habakkuk 1:13, which says, *"Your eyes are too pure* [holy] *to look upon evil, and You cannot look upon wickedness with favor.*" But if we read the context, which in this case, is just the rest of the verse, it says, *"So why do You look with favor on those who deal treacherously?"* Habakkuk was simply grappling with a fundamental misunderstanding of God's nature, assuming that because God is holy or perfect, He shouldn't be able to look upon sin and evil. But according to Scripture, He does (e.g., Gen.6:5; Prov.5:21-23; Heb.4:13)! The same was true for Jonah, who expected and even *wanted* God to wipe out the Ninevites! He actually even *complained* and wanted to *die* over his anger and frustration for God showing mercy and compassion to such wicked people (Jonah 4:2-3)!

While most Christians believe the Father and Son share the same essence and nature, many still see them as a "good cop - bad cop" duo. Our Father Yahweh is the "bad" or angry cop who is waiting for us to screw up so He can "open a can of Rambo" on us, unleashing His wrath, fury, and indignation, while Jesus, the Son, is the "good cop" who steps in to change His Father's mind, saying, *"Please Daddy, don't punish or wipe them out! Pour out Your wrath and indignation on ME and kill ME instead!"* We won't take time to expound on it here because it would take a separate book to do it justice, but such thinking is totally unbiblical! Yeshua said He and the Father are ONE, and that whoever sees Him has seen the Father (John 14:7-11). Contrary to popular belief, Yeshua was not abandoned by His Father on the cross. He clearly said, *"He who sent Me is WITH Me and has NOT left Me alone,* and told His disciples that, *"behold, an hour is coming and has already come for each of you to be scattered to his own home and to leave me alone, and yet I AM NOT ALONE because the Father is WITH Me."* The Father didn't "jump" out of the Son during His crucifixion, and their oneness was not temporarily suspended while He was dying. If so, the triune nature of God, as Father, Son, and Spirit, would have imploded! And how could they be one who share the exact same nature if the SON could take on our sin, but not the Father - who was apparently not even able to *look* at His Son! When the Lord cried out on the cross, *"My God, My God, why have you forsaken Me?"*, He wasn't saying the Father *literally* forsook Him. How could that happen if the Son and Father are truly ONE and Yeshua is God in the flesh? 2 Corinthians 5:19 clearly says *GOD was IN Christ, reconciling the world to Himself, not counting their sins against them.* As the Son of Man, the Lord was identifying with all of humanity, when we are experiencing our darkest hour, feeling alone and abandoned by God. Did you know Yeshua was quoting Psalms chapter 22, where David was expressing *his* feelings that God had forsaken *him?* And did you know that Psalms 22 is actually played out on the cross? We could take the time to look at it here, but I'll let you read it for yourself and be amazed!

It is vital to understand that Yeshua did not die *for* you or *because* of you; rather, He died AS you. In a mysterious or mystical way, you were right there with Him on the cross! And He didn't die to change the *Father's* mind about you or to convince Him to love and accept you in spite of your sin. Yahweh *never* changes and doesn't need to change because He is perfect in every way (Mal.3:6; Num.23:19). Yeshua or Jesus gave His life to change and transform YOU; He died to change YOUR mind about the Father, not the Father's mind about you. Sin not only mars how you see yourself – it also distorts how you see God, causing you to see and think of Him as your *enemy* (as we just saw in Colossians 1:21). Because sin brings you into guilt, shame, and a condemned conscience, you think you have to separate and distance *yourself* from God. However, it never causes GOD to separate or distance Himself from *you!* When God knew Adam and Eve had sinned, THEY withdrew from God – God did not withdraw from them; while THEY sought to hide themselves in shame, God actually came *looking* for Adam, didn't He? Of course, God knew where Adam was, but Adam didn't know where *Adam* was because his sin had blinded him. And when God commanded them to leave the Garden, contrary to what we've been taught, He wasn't "giving them the boot" out of anger and disgust, but out of love and mercy. It was a loving and merciful thing to have them leave and never return because if they had eaten from the Tree of Life in their fallen state, they would have lived forever in their fallen and blind state!

Do not misunderstand. God's Spirit is surely *grieved* or *quenched* by sin and disobedience, but again, because of what Yeshua has done on our behalf, our sins do not separate *Him* from us; rather, our guilty conscience causes <u>us</u> to *separate ourselves* or withdraw from Him because we are convinced we've become His enemy or that He's disgusted with us. And when we identify and see ourselves as enemies of God who are *cut off* or *alienated* from Him, we inevitably give ourselves over to behavior that will align with that perceived false identity. Most believers may "know" they are not God's enemies in a *doctrinal* sense, and that He will never literally abandon them, but many still see themselves as "sinners" who are "too messed up," and as a result, believe the Lord is angry, frustrated, or "fed up" with them – seeing Him more like the "Godfather" than God their "Father." Now let us take a brief look at God's *ultimate goal* or objective in sending His Son.

CHAPTER 11

The Ultimate Goal of Calvary

In the beginning of the book, I said the goal of Calvary or Yeshua's blood was <u>not</u> simply to have our sins forgiven or so we could have our names written in the Book of Life and go to heaven. You might wonder what could be greater than being born-again or going to heaven. Our salvation is unspeakably glorious, as well as the knowledge or assurance that we will spend eternity with the Lord in His kingdom once we pass from this life, but His sacrifice was about so much more than that!! He didn't redeem us from our sin only to get us into heaven after we die; if securing a "seat" for us in heaven was the goal, why doesn't the Lord just snatch us up at the moment of our conversion? As He prayed for His followers in John 17:15: *"I do <u>not</u> ask that You take them <u>out</u> of the world, but that You would <u>keep them</u> from the evil one."* And in Matthew 6:11, He commands us to pray that His kingdom come, and His will be done <u>here on earth</u>, *as it is in heaven.* This means His aim in our salvation is to bring the realm of heaven or His kingdom back into *us,* as it originally was at creation, that He might restore and establish His domain in the *earth* through His people!

It is time for the Body of Messiah to understand that our Lord did not die to merely save us *from* something; He died and resurrected to save us *for* something. Most would say it was to have our names recorded in the Book of Life or to have assurance of going to heaven after we die. Of course, eternal life is a glorious part of it, but did you know that God has something even *greater* in mind? Did you know that securing a place for us in His kingdom was <u>not</u> the ultimate *goal* or *objective* of the cross of Calvary? Just like God's written Word points us to the end goal or prize and prepares our hearts to receive it, Yeshua's death and resurrection was not the end; rather, it was a means *to the end*. When Yeshua uttered His last words on the cross, "It is finished," He was referring to the assignment or mission for which He came – to give His life as a ransom (Mark 10:45; John 12:27). But at Calvary, the desire and purpose of the Father, Son, and Spirit was just stepping into high gear!

So, what exactly was the <u>ultimate</u> goal or objective of Yeshua's death, burial, and resurrection? What greater purpose could Yeshua's sacrifice serve than to provide forgiveness, redemption, healing, eternal life, etc.? We spoke earlier of how most of us as believers fight and strive <u>for</u> victory, not realizing that because of what Yeshua has accomplished, we are to fight *from* victory (in a position of rest). Similarly, most of us live from an *earth* towards heaven perspective or mentality, but because we have been raised up and seated with Yeshua in heavenly realms *now*, He has called us to live from <u>heaven</u> *towards earth*. That might sound weird, but it just means we are to be more conscious of the kingdom of heaven and of our heavenly citizenship rather than our earthly citizenship; it means we are to live with a greater awareness of the invisible and eternal realm than we are of the visible and temporal realm. Yes, it is surely a process of learning to live this way, but this is why Paul tells us to set our minds on things "above," <u>not</u> on things below, and to fix our eyes on things which are "unseen" and "eternal," <u>not</u> on that which is seen and temporary (2 Cor.4:18; Col.3:1-3). Now that we have access to the mind of Yeshua and have a sanctified imagination, we are to meditate upon our heavenly home, where we are *currently* "seated with Christ" (1 Cor.2:16; Phil.1:27; Eph.2:6). If we understand our true origin and the kingdom that governs us, we won't become a victim of the environment and circumstances which God has called us to transform. You see, our true citizenship and origin determines what governs and dominates our lives. If we are born-again or in Yeshua, and yet act as though *the world* is our home, what we see or experience in this realm will govern, confine, and limit us. And understand that the purpose of fixing our eyes on heaven or the unseen realm will <u>not</u> make us "so heavenly minded that we are of no earthly good", as many believe. If that happens, it's because we're being religious or "churchy". If we are truly living from <u>heaven</u> towards earth, from our relationship with the Lord and our spirit, being "heavenly minded" will make us of MUCH earthly good – to the degree that we release the atmosphere of heaven that dwells in us and is upon us, as Yeshua said in Luke 17:21, *"The kingdom of God* [heaven] *is <u>within</u> you."*

You may ask, what is the "atmosphere" or "realm" of heaven or God's kingdom? The realm of heaven is where the Lord's GLORY and manifest presence permeates the atmosphere and where His perfect will is done. Again, did not Yeshua command us to pray that His kingdom come and will be done <u>on earth</u> - *as it is in heaven?* While most of God's people are waiting to leave or escape this earth through the rapture, He is waiting for us to catch the revelation of who we are in Him so that we, His ambassadors, can begin carrying out our assignment of demonstrating and enforcing the realities of His kingdom *here!* And does He not say that the *increase* of His government (kingdom or rule) would *never* end, and that in the Last Days, the knowledge of His glory would cover the *earth* as the waters cover the sea? (Matt.6:11; Is.9:7;11:9) This won't happen by a "sovereign act of God"; it will happen as a result of His people walking intimately with Him (Dan.11:32). When He sent His Spirit to permanently indwell every believer in Acts 2, that was the "down payment" and first stage of the "restoration of all things" spoken of in Acts 3:21.

What exactly is Yahweh restoring? *He aims to fully restore the very atmosphere of heaven into the earth; He is restoring that which was lost in the Garden with Adam and Eve, which was the privilege of an experiential, intimate relationship with Yahweh and the privilege to carry, reflect, and steward His very presence, glory, image, and likeness in the earth!* To the degree that we apprehend this truth and revelation, to that same degree will God's will and purpose be done on earth as it is in heaven – through <u>us</u>, His vessels, or temples! Our union with the Lord is not merely positional or doctrinal. What is a "doctrinal union" anyway? Yes, our union is spiritual, because God and His Spirit are unseen, but that union is to be practically, tangibly, and visibly manifested in and through our lives. As long as our union with Him is confined to the pages of scripture as mere doctrine and head knowledge, we will not demonstrate and manifest His nature, glory, and kingdom.

And let us keep this important truth in mind: Your physical death is <u>not</u> your savior! What does that mean? We obviously should not have a death-wish, nor should we be covetous of those who have already died in the Lord, but because most of us see death as the doorway that ushers us into heaven and the presence of God, it is seen as a "savior" of sorts. However, the truth is that the death (and resurrection) of YESHUA has <u>already</u> raised us up and seated us in heavenly realms, and His shed blood has torn the veil, giving us access to the presence of God NOW! We may object: "But Scripture says *it is appointed once for man to die, and after this, to face judgment,* and that *while we are in the body, we are <u>absent</u> from the Lord."* (Heb.9:27; 2 Cor.5:6). Again, we cannot take verses out of context from the rest of Scripture. When Paul says we are "absent" from the Lord as long as we're in our bodies, he's simply saying we aren't with Him in a full, literal, and face-to-face sense, but he also writes that we are not only "with" Him <u>now</u>, we are ONE spirit with Him. And concerning Hebrews 9, Paul says we have *already* died by our union with Yeshua and that we are currently *hidden in Him* in the Father (1 Cor.6:17; Rom.6; Col.3:1-3)! And if we are in the Lord, our sins have *already* been judged, as the very next verse in Hebrews says, *Christ also, having been offered <u>once</u> to bear the sins of many, will appear a second time for salvation <u>without reference to sin</u>, to those who eagerly await Him.* We may physically die one day, but we don't have to wait until then to walk in freedom over sin and temptation (and sickness and disease)! Neither do we have to wait until physical death to enjoy the presence of God and the realms of heaven. If being <u>currently</u> "seated in heavenly places" as "citizens" of heaven has no practical application in our lives while on earth, then such words are merely religious feel-good platitudes.

Ok – I just "let the cat out of the bag" and said it! Yes, as citizens of heaven, we have access to our true home NOW by our union with Yeshua (of course, by our spirit-man)! If people like Isaiah, Paul, and John had heavenly experiences, visitations, or encounters, why can't any other believer? God is no respecter of persons, and *all* things are possible for him who believes, right? When Yeshua said in John 10:9, *"I am the door* (not death); *if anyone enters through Me, he shall be saved, and <u>shall go in and out</u>, and find pasture,* what do you think He meant? He wasn't talking about gaining and losing our salvation or being in Him one day and out of Him the other, but about accessing heavenly realms.[37] We know the Lord's Spirit permanently dwells within us, but He said in John 17:24, *"Father, I desire, that those whom Thou has given Me, may <u>be with Me where I am</u>, that they may behold My glory.* He also said in John 14:21 that if we keep His commands and love Him, He will *disclose, reveal, or manifest Himself to us!* We may have read such passages a thousand times without seeing them in this light, but that's the way the Word of God is – there are multiple layers and nuggets of truth and revelation we can find if we dig past the surface meaning. Anyhow, this is another topic altogether, so we'll get back to the subject of *this* book!

Let's Get Practical!

Practically speaking, how does God prove, demonstrate, and manifest His kingdom and nature in and through our lives? Again, it all goes back to intimacy and relationship. But for many of us, even that might beg the question: how do we really become "intimate" with the Lord? All of us will readily agree that we should seek an intimate walk with the Lord, but many of us aren't sure how to go about making that a growing reality. We know it involves the basics such as reading and meditating on Scripture (and certainly obeying it), prayer, worship, and regularly gathering with other believers, but sometimes these spiritual disciplines can become more like a routine or tradition for us, where we can faithfully practice them for many years and yet still be quite shallow or superficial in our relationship with the Lord. We may truly love Him, desire to glorify Him, and seek to walk in obedience to His commands, but we still feel there's something missing in our relationship with Him. If you're like me, you were taught and led to believe that having your "devotional" or "quiet time" and going to church was all there was to it concerning your relationship with God. But brothers and sisters, there is SO much more we have access to concerning intimacy with the Lord and walking in the realities of His kingdom!

Elaborating on this would require a separate book, but for now I just want to focus on the ONE THING I believe is the most powerful and life-transforming thing we can do in our pursuit of intimacy with the Lord. Don't miss this because it's so simple – as the most profound and life-altering things we can do are oftentimes the *simplest* things. What am I talking about? Here it is: ***Waiting upon the Lord and practicing stillness and quietness before Him.*** Really, that's it? Yes, that's it. If we think worship is more important, we must realize that waiting upon the Lord and being still before Him *is* a form of worship. Of course, <u>all</u> that we do should be an expression of worship, I believe practicing stillness in the Lord's presence and fixing our gaze upon Him with the eyes of our hearts (contemplative or meditative prayer) is one of the highest forms of worship we can offer God.

However, waiting upon the Lord in this way has not only become a lost practice in this day and age, but is seen as pointless or superfluous. This is likely because "waiting" doesn't feel productive or that we're accomplishing anything; for others, the discipline of waiting before God in stillness makes them nervous (yes, it takes "discipline" because our flesh does <u>not</u> like sitting still or being quiet!). This is why most believers don't take time for it or don't recognize the value and reward it brings. What reward? Above all, its where we cultivate a deeper level of intimacy with the Lord and where greater transformation takes place, as He discloses Himself to us in deeply personal and even supernatural ways (see John 14:21). As Paul said, when we practice beholding, contemplating, and meditating on His glory with the eyes of our hearts, we are transformed into His image more and more (2 Cor.3:18). It's where God renews our hope, peace, and courage; its where we find safety and healing to our hearts or souls; its where the Lord grants us wisdom, counsel, guidance, and strength.[38] God tells us in Isaiah 30:15: *"in repentance and <u>rest</u> you will be <u>saved</u>, in <u>quietness</u> and <u>trust</u> is your <u>strength</u>, but you were not willing."* Remember, "repentance" isn't always about confessing and turning away from sin; it means a change of *mind* and *heart*, which <u>leads</u> to a change in our behavior or how we live. Repentance involves learning to see things from God's perspective and doing things *His* way, not ours.

It's not that we can't truly know Him or walk with Him and be used for His glory without regularly waiting upon Him in stillness and quietness. The point is, again, that this discipline is the door to greater transformation and deeper realms of intimacy with Him that cannot be accessed any other way. I don't know about you, but while

I am very thankful for what I have, I am *not* satisfied with my current level of intimacy with the Lord, and <u>nothing</u> in me wants to *remain* where I am. I yearn for an ever-growing *experiential* knowledge of my Lord and continually "press in" for a greater revelation and awareness of His presence, love, holiness, power, wisdom, etc.- *not* so I can serve Him better, but so I can KNOW <u>Him</u> better. Even the Apostle Paul, who surely knew the Lord deeply, expressed his deep desire and yearning to <u>know</u> Him much more, and he expressed this in the final days of his life and after all that he had experienced and accomplished in the Lord! Do we have that kind of hunger and thirst to go deeper with the Lord, or are we content to stay where we are? Yeshua said in John 17:3 that eternal life is all about knowing *Him*, not knowing *about* Him, serving Him, or even going to heaven. He said this because <u>all</u> that we do for Him and His kingdom is to *flow out of intimacy* with Him, amen? In other words, "being" comes before "doing," or *doing* flows out of *being* (at least that's the way God intended it to be).

I want to share another very practical thing we can do that will bring about transformation to our lives. We have already discussed the power of confessing God's Word over ourselves, but let me give you a specific and powerful example of that: As we begin our day and prepare to retire for the night, we all look in a mirror. Before or after your normal routine of grooming and cleaning, take a moment to look directly into your eyes, with focused intention, and speak God's Word or truth to yourself. You may have placed your favorite Bible verses on the mirror, around the house, or on the dashboard of your car, but have you ever verbally declared God's Word to yourself *in the mirror?* Your knee-jerk reaction to that idea may remind you of the self-worship of Narcissus, a mythical character in classic literature who was obsessed with his own reflection or appearance. But this is *far* from what we're talking about here. This is about agreeing with what your <u>Creator</u> and <u>Savior</u> has said about you in His Word, and *declaring* it to yourself with intention and conviction, which is the opposite of pride or arrogance. It actually requires *humility* to not only acknowledge who God says you are, but especially to <u>believe</u> and <u>confess</u> it. It is the pride of *false* humility that would belittle, minimize, or even reject the truth of who you are in Yeshua. Speaking God's truth over yourself in a mirror might feel strange, but as previously noted, if we're already practicing "self-talk" throughout the day, most of which is negative, why not use your tongue to bring life and blessing rather than death or destruction and curses? If you're going to eat the fruit of your lips, why not let that fruit be sweet? Remember, the Bible says we are transformed into the Lord's image as we behold His glory *as in a mirror* (2 Cor.3:18). In other words, Yeshua (and His Word) are like a mirror we look into to see who we are in HIM! So, when we see ourselves in a mirror, knowing we are one spirit with Him, we are not only looking at ourselves, but our Lord who fashioned us and indwells us!

If you decide to begin practicing this, you may feel hypocritical about some of the things you confess over yourself as your weaknesses and shortcomings come to mind. For instance, as you confess: "I am the righteousness of God in Christ" (2 Cor.5:21), you might be tempted to think, *"Yeah right!"* or, *"THIS is what righteousness looks like? Considering all my issues and the sin I still struggle with, there's NO way that verse can be true about <u>me</u>!"* And if you say, "By the stripes of Yeshua, I was and I AM healed" (Is. 53:5; Matt.8:17; 1 Pet.2:24), while you are currently battling a disease or symptoms that say otherwise, you may be tempted to think, *"I'm <u>lying</u> to myself - how can I say I AM healed when my body (or the doctor) says I'm <u>not</u>?"* But we already addressed this. Remember, when we declare something based on God's will for our lives that we are not *currently* experiencing or walking in, that is <u>not</u> lying, but *calling it forth by faith.* As we already discussed, God doesn't call things that are as though they *aren't* (that would be lying or denying reality)*;* rather, He calls things that <u>aren't</u> (in the visible realm) *as though they are.* And because <u>you</u>, who are fashioned in His image and likeness, are commanded to imitate Him, and to walk by faith rather than by sight, then it is not only acceptable, but His perfect and pleasing <u>will </u>for you to AGREE with what His Word says about you and to DECLARE or CONFESS it over yourself (Rom.4:17; Eph.5:1; 2 Cor.4:13; Rom.10:10). Isn't that what Mary did when Gabriel told her she was going to conceive Yeshua even though she had never been with a man? When Gabriel told her the Holy Spirit would bring about the conception, she said, *"May it be done to me according to your word!"* In other words, God's Word through the angel was first *spiritually* conceived or received in Mary's *heart* before the *physical* conception and manifestation could take place. And as noted earlier in this book, what did Yeshua say to many of those He healed? *"Let it be done to you AS you have believed,"* or, *"ACCORDING to your faith, may it be done unto you!"*

So, when you declare God's Word or truth over yourself, even when you aren't currently walking in it, but you truly believe it nonetheless, as Yeshua said in Mark 11:22-24, you WILL have it, or it WILL become your reality! The key is *conceiving* it in your heart and "seeing" it with your spiritual eyes. As long as you do this, you obviously don't need a mirror in the equation for His will to become a reality, but there's something powerful about looking into your own eyes while speaking God's Word over yourself. You might even get a few "Holy Ghost Goosebumps" or feel His presence when you do it, because remember, He dwells *within* you! And NO, it doesn't make you "fleshly" if you get emotional or feel excited concerning your walk with God – as Romans 14:17 clearly says the kingdom of God is not meat and drink, but righteousness, PEACE, and JOY in the Holy Spirit (which means two thirds of God's kingdom involve our emotions)!

Sons and Lovers Vs. Servants and Workers

Most Christians strive to live FOR the Lord as His servant, worker, or slave who is motivated by duty or a need to perform and accomplish, rather than living FROM Him as a son and friend motivated by love, intimacy, and desire. Yes, we are to live "for" the Lord and serve Him, but rather than doing so out of a sense of religious duty, routine, and discipline, He would have us do so out of an intimate relationship with Him rooted in love. If we are serving Yeshua *from* or *out of* our relationship with Him, it is impossible *not* to do much <u>for</u> Him and His kingdom, but it is surely possible that we can serve Him without having a close or deep relationship with Him. If we are a type-A or driven and task-oriented person, God can certainly use us for His kingdom purposes, but keep in mind that while "workers" or laborers may accomplish much, those who focus on a *love relationship* with God will far outwork the workers because they are motivated and empowered by <u>love</u> and the <u>Spirit</u> rather than a drive to produce or accomplish.

Obviously, type-A driven people can also be motivated by their love for God, but the point is, while we indeed "serve" the Lord and labor for His kingdom, He does not "need" our service, as Acts 17:25 says <u>isn't</u> served by human hands in the sense that He has any deficiencies or needs we can meet; He created us because He *desires* <u>relationship</u> and <u>intimacy</u> with us, and desires that all our labor, service, and work for His kingdom purposes flow *out* of that intimacy and a position of *rest,* as opposed to toiling or striving (e.g., an analogy we've all heard from Luke 10: are we a "Mary" or a "Martha"?). He said we will bear much fruit if we abide in *Him,* not His written Word or laws. Surely we are to meditate on His Word or commands and observe them, as it pleases Him and brings us great reward or blessing, but He calls us to "be" still or cease striving, and *know* <u>Him</u>, for it is out of our intimate knowledge of Him that we will "do" great exploits in His Name and power (Ps.1:2,19:11,46:10; Dan.11:32).

Just as grace naturally compels us to obey Him and live holy, so intimacy with God naturally compels us to advance His kingdom and fulfill His will in HIS power. We must keep in mind that our identity is never to be found in our service to God or our giftings and callings; we are His *sons* before we are His *servants,* as service is to flow out of sonship. Servants or slaves must be told what to do, but sons and lovers who know their identity in the Lord *know* what to do because they share His heart and mind, being led by His Spirit rather than the Law or a "to do list." Of course, as we continue to seek His face and heart, learning to live this way is a process and we will never fully "arrive" or do it perfectly 24/7! We've already touched on this, but I believe THE key to becoming a son who is driven by desire and love (versus a servant or worker driven by duty and performance) is this: REST. Dr James Richards writes:

Effortless change is impossible when it is sought through behavior modification. You may change the behavior, but inwardly it always requires effort. Then on a day that you are too tired or too frustrated to put forth the effort, you find yourself rebounding into the old destructive behaviors. It is this continual trying and failing that finally persuades your heart that change is just too hard. When you believe change is just too hard, the only remaining solution is to justify the very behavior that is robbing you. There will always be some effort involved in change. The question is, <u>will it be the wasted effort of trying to control your behavior or the fruitful effort of changing your beliefs</u>? The New Testament (Heb.4) puts forth an interesting paradox: "Labor to enter into rest." At a casual glance this seems like a contradictory concept. If you're laboring, then you're not resting. So it becomes obvious that <u>the labor is the process of persuading your heart to believe</u> (or have faith). *Once* *a new belief is installed, the laboring or striving is over. From that point on, you're on automatic pilot. The change is effortless; Installing the belief was the place of effort!......Both success and failure require the same effort. It is not even the believing that is hard. The only thing that is hard is trying to change your behavior without changing your beliefs!* (Dr James Richards; *Wired for Success, Programmed for Failure,* Milestones International Publishing, pp.145-146)

In other words, your only "work" is to REST and to BELIEVE the Gospel! If you are in Yeshua or Christ, IT IS FINISHED – the work is DONE! You are COMPLETE in Him. As we read in Isaiah 26:12, *Lord, You establish peace for us, since You <u>have performed for us all our works</u>!* And as we have seen throughout this book, this rest will fuel, inspire, and empower you to flesh out your identity in the Lord as one who is whole, righteous, holy, and healed! We have also seen that while we are a "finished product" in the Lord's eyes, manifesting the fullness of our identity in Him is a *process* that involves renewing our minds so that who we are outwardly will increasingly reflect who we *already* are inwardly.

In closing, a huge reason many of us have little to no impact on the world and our culture is not only due to our lack of identity, but also our skewed understanding of eschatology (doctrine concerning the Last Days or End Times). Most of us have adopted a fatalistic and deterministic view of the Last Days, which has caused a spirit of laziness, passivity, and indifference to pervade the Body of Christ. Surely you have heard the saying: *all that is needed for evil to prevail is for righteous men to do nothing.* But why would the "righteous" do nothing or not act? There are many reasons, but I believe one of them is this: in Matthew chapter 24, Yeshua prophesies many terrible events leading up to His return, basically saying things will "go to Hell" in the world, and because many of us have come to believe that He will "snatch us up" before things get really bad, we watch things unravel from the sidelines without much concern or involvement.

Mostly on a subconscious level, we let sin and evil prevail around us, reasoning that because the Lord said these things would happen in the end days, why should we fight *against* it – because even if we *do*, it will happen anyway, right? Yahweh's purposes will indeed be fulfilled concerning the Last Days, but that does not give us an excuse to sit on our spiritual (and physical) backsides and not care that the world "goes to Hell in a hand basket" while we watch from heaven. Whether or not the Bride of Yeshua will be raptured or physically taken off the earth *before* the Great Tribulation is not the point or question.[39] What matters is that we have allowed the truth that things will "go to Hell" before the Lord's return to lull us into a spiritual apathy, indifference, and even lukewarmness and compromise. Also, spiritual laziness and negligence sets in because we are convinced we won't be here when things get that bad – so why "prepare"? Aren't we supposed to *look forward* to the day of our redemption and eagerly *long* for His appearance? Of course, but many have developed an escapist mentality, becoming selfishly focused on their own redemption or salvation, losing their passion for reaching the lost and making a difference in society. Others have even become apathetic about forsaking sin and living holy lives. Rather than believing they can live in victory over sin and temptation *now,* they confine it to the time they "cross the Jordon" and get to the "sweet by and by." Yeshua asked whether He would find *faith* on the earth upon His return and that in the Last Days, the love of many will grow *cold* (Luke 18:8; Matt.24:12). Those words apply to believers as much as they do to unbelievers, as the Lord admonished the Church in the book of Revelation for leaving Her first love and becoming spiritually lukewarm and even *dead!* Let us do everything we can, by His empowering grace and love, to be sure we do not fall in the category of faithlessness and cold heartedness! We all want to hear, *"Well done, good and faithful servant; enter into the joy of your Master!"* (Matt.25:21)

We ask again: what does this have to do with overcoming sin and temptation or walking in holiness? Just like our relationship with God's Word and Law, it has *everything* to do with it! This book has clearly shown how our beliefs, doctrines or theology can affect our walk of faith and how we engage the world around us. We have all heard the sayings, "What you don't know can't hurt you," and "Ignorance is bliss," but we have seen that ignorance can not only harm us, but wreak havoc in our lives and even *destroy* or *kill* us (Hos.4:6; Prov.29:18). Mistaking lies or falsehood for truth is even worse, as Proverbs 14:12 says *there is a way that <u>seems</u> right to a man, but its end is the way of <u>death</u>,* and remember, the Lord did <u>not</u> say the truth will set us free; He said *knowing* the truth will set us free (John 8:32).

In other words, truth and vision infuse us with a renewed sense of purpose, strength, faith, courage, and commitment, and above all, a deep desire to take action. And as we covered earlier, we are *transformed* by the renewing of our <u>mind</u>, and by faith we identify with Galatians 2:21, *"I have been crucified with Yeshua; it is no longer I who live, but Yeshua who lives in me, and the life I live in the body, I live by faith in the Son of God who loved me and gave His life for me!"* As we grow in our revelation of who the Lord is in us and who we are in Him, those "glimmering lights of Egypt" that once turned our heads, diluting and defiling our affection for Him, will increasingly become detestable to us, and we will find ourselves naturally and effortlessly walking out our true identity and inheritance in Him!

End Notes

---

[1] Paul quotes these verses in Romans 3:10-12: Many Christians say these verses apply to them as believers, which is bad enough, but hopefully they do <u>not</u> believe verses 13-18 also apply to them! It says they are "liars whose mouths are full of cursing and bitterness," that their "feet are quick to shed blood," that "destruction and misery are in their paths," and that they have "no peace" and "no fear of God in their eyes"! This sounds like a perfect description of someone who *does not* know God or who has not been born-again – or worse, like an *evil* or *wicked* person!

[2] As we mature in our faith and understanding of the Word, the Lord will continue to show us how backwards our thinking is in some areas. For instance, when Yeshua spoke of fasting in the gospels, He assumed we would do it because He said "when" you fast, but most of the Church says "if" we fast. And when John says "if" anyone sins, we say "when" we sin, implying it is something we should *expect* because we're "only human" and sin "all the time".

[3] This verse suggests "God's people" can be "sinners," although it is to be rendered, "sinners <u>among</u> My people." First, even if it were true that sinners (those who practice sin) can belong to God, it says such people will "die by the sword," which means Yahweh is serious when it comes to living in sin – especially if we claim to be His people! Secondly, Romans 9:6-8 says, *For they are <u>not all</u> Israel who are descended from Israel, <u>neither</u> are they all children because they are Abraham's descendants, but through Isaac your descendants will be named; that is, it is <u>not</u> the children of the flesh who are children of God, but the children of the <u>promise</u> are regarded as descendants.* (See also Matt.3:9; Rom.2:29; John 8:39). This obviously includes the Church: not all physical members of a church are true *spiritual* members simply because they call themselves members of His Body and are among the congregation or even preach from the pulpit.

[4] This does <u>not</u> mean we are carnal if we *desire* to experience the Lord in ways that engage our physical senses. The question is, are experiences *required* for us to have true faith? When Yeshua said, "Blessed are those who have believed and yet have *not* seen," He obviously <u>wasn't</u> saying those who *haven't* experienced the Lord in supernatural ways are *more* blessed than those who have; He was drawing a distinction between those who *require* their physical senses to be engaged in order to have faith (like Thomas did), versus those who have faith *regardless* of whether

or not they physically see, hear, or feel anything from God. The same applies to Yeshua's words when He said, "an evil and adulterous generation seeks after a sign" (Matt.12:39). The context shows that those who asked for a sign were unwilling to take Yeshua at His Word, requiring a miracle in order to believe.

[5] It is important to note that when the Bible uses the term, "flesh," it can refer to either <u>sinful/worldly appetites</u> or desires (the spiritual), or it can refer to the <u>body</u> (the physical). Differentiating between the two in any given context is important.

[6] While Yeshua "exists in the form of God," is the "exact representation of His nature," and "all the fullness of deity indwells Him," He humbly and *willingly* laid aside or suspended His God-powers and privileges while on earth, submitting Himself to the frailty and limitations of His own creation (Col.2:9; Heb.1:3; Phil.2:6-8).

[7] Scripture says God does use evil to ultimately bring about His purposes for His glory (e.g., Rom.8:28; Gen.50:20), but saying He sovereignly <u>uses</u> it for His purposes and glory is totally different than saying sin or evil *itself* glorifies Him, that He created it, and intentionally *causes* it. If Yeshua said a kingdom divided against itself cannot stand, that means God would be working against His own will and desires by creating or causing sin and evil while at the same time sending His Son to *destroy* it.

[8] "But isn't exaggeration lying"? It depends on our motive or intention. If we're trying to make ourselves look good or to persuade and coerce someone to think a certain way so that we may gain some advantage, then yes, exaggeration is wrong or sinful. But if we're simply trying to make a point or to help someone better understand what we're saying, using exaggeration or hyperbole is perfectly fine. For instance, Yeshua used exaggeration when He said we should "cut off our hand" or "gouge our eye out" if it causes us to sin – but we would all be blind and dismembered if we took Him literally!

[9] Because Yeshua is the embodiment of the invisible God and is one in essence, being and purpose with the Father, it was *impossible* for Yeshua to desire and act out of alignment the Father's mind or will. If this is so, why did He make such statements? The same reason He was baptized. Yeshua didn't need baptism as we do, as it symbolizes the washing away of our sin and old nature, but He was baptized as an example for us to follow – just as He gave us the example of complete surrender to the Father's will even though He and the Father (and Spirit) are, and will forever be, one in essence and being.

[10] Yeshua did say in John 12:25, *"He who hates his life in this world will keep it to eternal life,"* but He wasn't saying we are to literally hate *ourselves* or to even hate our life, as He gave us physical (and spiritual) life, and commands us to love others AS we love *ourselves*. He said we are to hate our lives "in this world," meaning we are to continually remind ourselves that we are citizens of heaven who cannot be friends with the world by sharing its values and ideology. (1 John 2:15; Jam.4:4).

[11] Does this mean an unbeliever or immature Christian is *incapable* of keeping any of God's laws? Of course not. Paul is talking about having a *pure* motive to not only keep God's laws, but do so *naturally, joyfully,* and for the *love* and *glory of God.* People can do a decent job of keeping certain laws God established, but if it isn't rooted in love for Him, the Bible calls such works "dead works."

[12] For Further study concerning how God's grace and love inspire or empower us to walk in obedience to His laws, read the following verses: John 14:15,21; James 2:17; 1 John 2:3-6, 3:19, 5:2-3; Rom.3:31, 16:26; 1 Cor.9:21, 15:10; 2 Cor.3:6, 5:14; Gen.6:8, Ch.18, 33:11; Ex.22:27, 33:12,19, 33:19, 34:6; Lev.26:44; Num.6:25, 14:18; Deut.4:29-39, 30:3; Ezek.33:11-20; 2 Sam.24:14; 2 Kings 13:23; 2 Chron.30:9; Neh.9:17,31; Is.30:18,19, 60:10; Ps.51:1, 86:5,15, 111:4, 112:4, 116:5, 145:8-9; Jer.31:2; Zec.4:6; Dan.9:9, 9:18; Ezra 9:8; Zeph.3:15; Jon.4:2; Ps.84:11, 119:142,160.

[13] Yahweh spoke much more about the circumcision of the hearts than of the flesh. (e.g., Lev.26:41; Deut.10:16,30:6; Jer.4:4, 9:25-26; Rom.2:28-29). Circumcision of the heart, which the Lord began *before* Yeshua came, is what gives us the desire and ability to keep His commands. Until our fleshly, sin-loving heart is replaced with the nature of Yeshua, keeping the commands or laws of Yahweh will not only be hard or difficult, but *impossible* – that is, in the manner that glorifies the Lord (e.g., our motive being love, not duty, and our source of power being the Holy Spirit and not our flesh or will power and self-resolve).

[14] We discussed this at the beginning of the book, but most Christians have memorized verses like Jeremiah 17:9, which tells us "the heart is deceitful, wicked and desperately sick." Again, if we are born-again Spirit filled believers who have become new creations in Yeshua and are one spirit with Him, we didn't just have our hearts *changed;* we had a "heart transplant" (see Ezek.11:19, 18:31, 36:26; Jer.31:33). This verse only applies to UNbelievers or those who remain spiritually dead, lost, corrupt, and in bondage to their sin nature! If you are ONE with Christ,

have been given a NEW heart, and you share in God's divine nature, how could your heart be evil, sick, and wicked? All Scripture is God-breathed, but this is one example how not all Scripture applies to *every* individual in *every* circumstance and time (this should be obvious, but it apparently isn't).

[15] Most Christians believe that when Yeshua said He "fulfilled" the Law in Matthew 5:17, it means He did away with it, abolished it, or made it null and void. But if that were so, the Lord would have contradicted Himself by saying: "I did not come to abolish the Law, but to *abolish* the Law." The Greek word for *fulfill,* pleroo, means to "fully preach" or to "fill up," which means Yeshua came to fully or rightly preach God's Law, and fulfill its true purpose in the spirit of grace and truth, as John 1:17 says (as opposed to legalism and duty).

[16] I personally believe this means the brightness of God's manifest glory and light upon them totally faded away, because remember, the Bible says that by our union with the Lord, we are not only children and <u>sons of light</u>, but that we <u>are</u> light; it also says we have been "crowned" with God's glory and that His glory has arisen upon us. See 1 Thess.5:5; Eph.5:8 John 8:12, 14:20-23, 17:22, Matt.5:14, Heb.2:7; Is.60:1-4. I hear of testimonies of believers *today* who have been seen <u>literally</u> shining with God's glory, and I believe this is where the Lord is taking His people in these last days. When Isaiah 60:2 actually says His glory *will be seen upon us,* that isn't confined to the *spiritual* but includes the <u>physical</u> (like it did with Moses), and because we live under a superior covenant through Yeshua, we certainly shouldn't expect *less* than what Old Testament saints had! God's manifest glory or light is just one way He will make the "knowledge" of His glory "cover the earth as the waters cover the sea"! (Hab.2:14)

[17] Most Christians have no problem with believing we look just like our Savior (in the spirit) and WILL look just like Him when we see Him, but they cry "heresy!" at the belief that we will look just like Yahweh or the Father (even though they admit that Yeshua is the "spitting image" of His Father)!

[18] This is confined to God's Law concerning morality or behavior – <u>not</u> the leading of His Spirit in everyday life. Even Yeshua said He only did and said what He saw the Father doing and saying (John 5:19,12:49).

[19] Let it be clear: we are <u>not</u> saying <u>Faith + Works = Salvation</u> or that we are saved by our faith *and* obedience. We truly are saved by grace through faith ALONE, however, if the faith we profess is genuine or a work of the Holy Spirit, it not only saves us, but it will always bear the fruit of good works or obedience. In

other words, works don't produce or procure our salvation; faith <u>alone</u> produces salvation, which in turn yields or leads to our obedience or good works. This means salvation and works are inseparably connected. So, if there was a "formula", it would be this: <u>Faith = Salvation + Works</u>.

[20] These words of Paul affirm or validate Jeremiah 6:10,16, where Yahweh's people "cannot listen" to His Word and say, "we will not walk in it" because His Word or Law has become "an object of scorn" which they take "no pleasure in." If you are interested in going into more detail on God's Law and how we are to relate with it (and <u>not</u> relate with it), please see my book entitled, *God's Law & the Believer's Walk of Faith*.

[21] This touches on Colossians 1:24, where Paul speaks of his sufferings or hardships *"filling up that which is lacking in Christ's afflictions."* The sufferings of Yeshua are <u>not</u> "lacking" in the sense they are insufficient or deficient when it comes to purchasing our redemption, sanctification, or salvation. What Paul is saying is that because Yeshua is no longer here in a physical or literal way, the world no longer has Him as a visible picture or presentation of the Father's nature or character (e.g., His holiness, love, mercy, grace, wisdom, power, etc.). In *this* sense the Lord's sufferings are "lacking". But Paul says in the proceeding verses that because Yeshua lives IN us and His Spirit works THROUGH us in the midst of our own sufferings for His Name and the gospel, the world *does* have a picture of the Father – and so in this way, we have the privilege of "completing" or "filling up what is lacking" in His sufferings.

[22] More Christians are coming to understand that the practice of meditation is <u>not</u> "New Age" or something we should avoid and fear. The fact is, meditation is GOD'S idea, and He *command* us to meditate or "dwell" upon certain things, namely His Word, along with that which is true, good, lovely, etc. (e.g., Phil.4:8; Ps.1:2, 4:4, 63:6, 119:23). The truth is, ALL of us meditate, whether we realize it or not. Meditation is simply thinking or contemplating deeply about something or dwelling on particular thoughts and ideas – be it positive/holy things or negative/evil things.

[23] Notice it says as a man thinks in his HEART, not his mind. Why? Because this verse is talking about the inner convictions of our heart or spirit, not what we mentally or intellectually believe and think.

[24] Science has proven that the atom is composed of only 0.00001% physical matter, which clearly means we, as well as the material universe, are composed of over 99% energy. What we *see* with our eyes would suggest the opposite, but the quantum, subatomic, or unseen realm says otherwise.

[25] 1 Corinthians 15:46 seems to say the opposite. Paul says: *However, the spiritual is not first, but the natural; then the spiritual.* Yes, but the context clearly tells us that Paul was <u>not</u> saying the natural realm came before the spirit realm or that the seen gave birth to the unseen (which of course would make no sense). Here is the context: *It is written, the first man, Adam, became a living soul. The last Adam [Yeshua] became a life-giving spirit. However, the spiritual is not first, but the natural; then the spiritual. The first man is born from the earth; the second man is from heaven.* Paul is simply saying the natural man, Adam, first came (to earth) before the spiritual man, Yeshua. Paul stated such an obvious point to build a framework for chapter 15, where he talks about the resurrection, where we, who were sown a perishable/natural body, will be raised with an *imperishable/spiritual* body. In this sense, the natural came first, *then* the spiritual. But Scripture also makes the case that God knew us *before* we were fashioned in our mother's womb, at least implying the speculative *possibility* that we existed solely as spirits before we took on a body. See also: Col.1:16; John 1:3; Rom.15:27; I Cor.9:11.

[26] This is precisely why we must be careful not to automatically reject something or label it "demonic" and "heretical" simply because we can't find a Bible verse to back it up. The point is <u>not</u> that we should believe something is of God just because it *doesn't* contradict His Word or nature, but that we should "test the spirits" and "examine all things", rather than quickly dismissing something or rejecting it because it's not in the Bible (see 1 John 4:1; 1 Thess.5:21). It seems many Christians believe it is "Father, Son and Holy *Bible*", rather than Father, Son, and Holy SPIRIT, *by whom* we test the spirits or examine all things!

[27] But what about Romans 11:33, where Paul says, *How unsearchable are His judgments and unfathomable His ways! For who has known the mind of the Lord or who became His counselor?* Is Paul contradicting himself? How can he say we have the mind of Yeshua and then make such a statement? When he says "we have the mind of Yeshua" or "know all things," he obviously isn't saying that because Yeshua lives in us, it means we know everything God knows or that all of our thoughts and ideas originate in God. We do not *physically* have the mind of Yeshua and *literally* know everything; Paul is simply saying we have <u>access</u> to His thoughts, mind, and knowledge by our union with Him. To the degree that we seek His heart and cultivate intimacy with Him, to the same degree will His Spirit enable us to know and prove His perfect will. Yeshua even said in John 16:13 that His Spirit would reveal to us the things which are to come (future events).

[28] Christians believe you're lying if you declare something that doesn't exist or that which isn't your current experience or reality. They say "you need to call it like it is," but if we are to be imitators of God and follow the model Yeshua set for us in His Word, we are to call *forth* or speak that which we *desire* to see (of course, with the stipulation that it agrees with the Word, nature, and will of God).

[29] Note: Yeshua tells us to speak to the <u>mountain</u> (or problem/obstacle), not to *God* <u>about</u> the mountain. Of course, until we mature in our faith and walk with the Lord, He invites us to talk with Him *about* the mountains or problems we encounter in life, but His desire is that we do not remain spiritual *babes* and that we step into our *sonship*, being awakened to the authority He has given us and use it for His glory (I Cor.3:1-2, 13:11, 14:20).

[30] Gaslighting is a form of psychological manipulation in which the abuser tries to sow self-doubt and confusion in their victim's mind. It is an effort to gain power and control over another person by distorting reality and forcing them to question their own judgment and intuition.

[31] I do <u>not</u> endorse this, but the book, *The Secret,* by Rhonda Byrne, focuses on the "law of attraction." It's main teaching is that nothing can come into our lives unless we "summon" or welcome it through persistent focus and thoughts. Thus, whether you are aware of it or not, all that surrounds you right now (good and bad) has been attracted to you. As you focus on what you desire, you change the vibration of atoms of those things so that they begin to align with your own vibration and manifest themselves in your life. Ultimately, you control or determine your own frequency or vibration so that you can "attract" things like health, wealth, peace, fulfillment, etc. The problem with this teaching is NOT that it reflects falsehood concerning the spiritual truths, laws, or axioms established by God. Much of it is actually based on biblical principles and spiritual/scientific axioms. The problem is that it is *divorced* from a relationship with our heavenly Father and makes *man* the center of everything – as though life is all about *us* and fulfilling *our* needs and desires. It also makes materialism the goal of life, but Yeshua said in Mark 8, *"What good is it for a man to gain the whole world and yet forfeit his soul; or what can man give in exchange for his soul?"* The law of attraction is a good example of how a person can benefit (in the natural) from respecting and observing certain laws God has established in the universe without knowing *Him.* Just as we can *illegally* use or *wrongly* relate with the laws of God, and ultimately reap condemnation and death, so we can illegally use the spiritual laws He established at creation.

[32] Of course there are times when the Lord says "no" or "not now" to something we are praying for – even if our desires are in alignment with His Word and nature. If He says no to something we have a scriptural "warrant" to pray for, it is not because He changed His mind or Word, but because He knows we aren't prepared (yet) to properly steward the answer or blessing, as Proverbs 20:21 says *an inheritance gained in a hurry at the beginning will not be blessed in the end.* In such cases, we must persevere in prayer, knowing the Lord will eventually grant us the desires of our hearts once He sees we are prepared to receive and properly steward the answer.

[33] There are a growing number of people who have been deceived and dangerously misled by the false teaching which says that because God dwells within us by His Spirit, we *become* Christ or that we <u>are </u>Christ, the anointed One. They refer to this as "Christ-consciousness," which, in this context, is clearly heretical. When Colossians 3:11b says "Christ is all and in all," it does <u>not</u> mean Christ *becomes* us or that we *become* Christ, but that all people groups or nations are included in Him concerning His atoning sacrifice and that He excludes *no* person, race, gender, nationality, etc. However, there is a way to be biblically "Christ-conscious," which is when we are more conscious or aware of HIM and His presence *in* us than we are of ourselves, as Colossians goes on to say in chapter 3, verse 3, *For you <u>died</u>, and your life is now <u>hidden</u> with Christ in God.* Paul also speaks about this in more detail in Romans chapters 6-8.

[34] It is important to note that Yeshua spoke of having faith "like" a mustard seed, <u>not</u> SMALL AS a mustard seed. He did say it was "smaller" than other seeds in Matthew 13:32, but the correlation between faith and a mustard seed was not about the <u>size</u> of the seed or the <u>amount</u> of faith we have. He used the analogy of the mustard seed because while it may be tiny, it is one of the most tenacious, persistent, and "stubborn" seeds – pushing up even through the toughest of barriers to produce its fruit. In other words, if our faith does not give up or give in to pressure or resistance LIKE or AS a mustard seed doesn't, our faith will be able to move mountains!

[35] Because God's gifts and calling are irrevocable or without repentance (Rom.11:29), it is possible for a believer to operate in the supernatural gifts of the Spirit, including miracles, while not living a lifestyle characterized by godliness and obedience. We may not understand this, but Yeshua made it clear in Matthew 7 that we can operate in the supernatural power of God without truly knowing Him. This proves that just because someone performs miracles or casts out demons does not mean they are intimate with God or that God endorses their lifestyle and doctrine. It is also important to understand that if a person has sin in their life or

they hold to false doctrine in certain areas, and yet healing miracles still happen through their lives, that does <u>not</u> mean Satan is using them and not God. This is where the gift of discerning of spirits is important (I Cor.12:10). We also do not want to use the excuse that because Satan does false signs/wonders, we should avoid *true* signs/wonders. Satan does not counterfeit or copy something that has little to no value, just as criminals do not make counterfeit $1 or $5 bills. This means *false* miracles do not negate *true* miracles; rather, they affirm and validate the existence of *genuine* or *authentic* miracles. If you are interested in learning more about the supernatural gifts of the Spirit (and experiences) and whether or not they are still valid for the Church today, please see my book entitled, *Super Natural Christianity* (on Amazon).

[36] Galatians 3:26 and Romans 8:14 say <u>all</u> believers are "sons" of God (spiritually, of course), just as Romans 2:29 says all believers are spiritually Jewish or of Israel. Because there is "neither male nor female; Jew nor Greek or Gentile" (Gal.3:27-28), the Bible can call female believers "sons" and male believers the "Bride."

[37] No, we aren't talking about the New Age practice of astral projection, but about the LORD escorting our spirit-man into the heavenlies. Those who practice astral projection are engaging in a demonic exercise, thereby opening themselves up to deception and bondage.

[38] Ps.62:5, 119:147; Prov.20:22; Is.40:31, 30:15; Lam.3:25; Micah 7:7

[39] Scripture shows that whenever Yahweh brings judgment, it is the *wicked* or *sinner* who is removed or taken– <u>not</u> the righteous. For example, Noah and his family were protected in the Ark (which represented Yeshua) while the flood took away <u>wicked</u>; the Israelites were protected by the blood of the Lamb on their doorposts *while* Yahweh's judgments destroyed and *removed* the <u>wicked</u> around them; at Korah's rebellion in the wilderness, the <u>wicked </u>were taken or removed, *not* the righteous; Righteous Lot and his family were led to safety *while* Yahweh took out or destroyed the <u>wicked</u>. Revelation 14 says that when the "harvest of the earth is ripe", an angel will remove the <u>wicked</u> from among the righteous. Yeshua affirmed this in Matthew 13:49. There is a good reason for this: the Lord says the *meek* or *gentle* shall inherit the earth, *not* the wicked (Ps.37:11; Matt.5:5); He destroys or eliminates the <u>wicked </u>from the earth, even the *memory* of them (Ps.21:10, 34:16, 104:35, 119:119); Yeshua says in Matthew 24:40, *"There will be two men in the field; one shall be taken and one shall be left,"* we have always assumed the one who is left is the *wicked*, but if that were true, it would break the clear

pattern we see in Scripture of the *righteous* remaining while the *wicked* are taken, or the *righteous* inheriting the earth rather than the wicked (just as Yeshua said in verse 39 that the *wicked* were taken from the earth at the time of Noah and the flood).